# HEART AND

GW00746016

# JONAH: RELUCTANT PROPHET, MERCIFUL GOD

# EXODUS: FROM SLAVERY TO SERVICE

## Andrew Facey

The Bible Reading Fellowship
OPENING THE BIBLE

Text copyright © Andrew Facey 1996

The author asserts the moral right to be
identified as the author of this work.

Published by
**The Bible Reading Fellowship**
Peter's Way, Sandy Lane West
Oxford OX4 5HG
ISBN 0 7459 3277 0
**Albatross Books Pty Ltd**
PO Box 320, Sutherland
NSW 2232, Australia
ISBN 0 7324 0954 3

First edition 1996
10 9 8 7 6 5 4 3 2 1 0

**Acknowledgments**
Unless otherwise stated, scripture is taken from
The New Revised Standard Version of the Bible
copyright © 1989 by the Division of Christian
Education of the National Council of the
Churches of Christ in the USA.

Scripture marked (NIV) taken from the Holy
Bible, New International Version, copyright ©
1973, 1978, 1984 by International Bible
Society. Used by permission of Hodder and
Stoughton Limited.

A catalogue record for this book is
available from the British Library

Printed and bound in Malta
by Interprint Limited

# Contents

*To my wife, Dr Jane Facey, whose sharp mind, penetrating comments, unfailing support and loving encouragement continue to be a blessing to me.*

# Acknowledgments

This material has all been 'road-tested' in a real, live church! My considerable thanks to the parish church of St John the Baptist, Egham, to Alistair Magowan, its Vicar, and to its Home Group Network, for allowing me the time to write this material and for being so gracious and encouraging in the use of it.

# Introduction

Welcome to this book of Home Group study material! Over the page, you will find some practical suggestions about how to use this material. Immediately after that, you will find an introductory chapter on how to lead a study group.

The studies in Jonah and those in Exodus are quite different from each other. It doesn't matter which you start with, but do think about it first. The paragraphs below will help you decide.

## Jonah: Reluctant prophet, merciful God

These studies take us through the whole of the book of Jonah, in five sessions. We look at Jonah as a story, a story about God, Jonah and various non-Jewish people. At times the action of the book centres upon God and Jonah, and then we concentrate on that relationship. We focus on God—his calling of Jonah and his dealings with him; and on Jonah—his response to God's call and his motives in so acting. At times the action centres upon Jonah's (and God's) dealings with non-Jewish sailors, kings and people, and then we concentrate on the three-cornered relationship between God, Jonah and these people, looking at issues of God's involvement with the peoples of the world and with his creation, and at the part Jonah is asked to play in the outworking of God's plans.

The book of Jonah is a delightful and carefully crafted story. For all its brevity, it raises substantial and fascinating questions about God's dealings with his world.

## Exodus: From slavery to service

Exodus is much larger and more sprawling than Jonah, so we study seven passages and not the whole book. The studies are all from the first part of Exodus, stopping at chapter 24. Again, we focus on God's dealings with his chosen people and with non-Jewish people, this time the Egyptians. The framework of these studies is the theme 'From Slavery to Service'. By exploring that theme, we chart Israel's release from bondage to Pharaoh and their entry into the service and the worship of God. By this means, we take a look at issues of slavery and oppression today, and ask what it means to be rescued out of slavery into God's service.

## How to use this study material

Each study session has:

• Study notes—leading group members through the session. This is normally only one double-page, but watch out. Occasionally it is more!

• Leader's notes—helping leaders prepare for each session and learn more about the Bible passage being studied.

Copyright permission is given for the study notes in this book to be photocopied for group use—so that each member may have a copy of the study notes to use and keep. The leader's notes and other contents of the book are excluded from this provision.

A space called 'Growth Points' is provided on each study notes where group members may write in anything they want to take away with them from that session.

We recommend that everyone has a copy of the study notes at the beginning so they can follow it through together. But that is entirely up to you. You may prefer to give it out at the end, so that members can refresh their memories later.

The translation used is generally The New Revised Standard Version (NRSV) or New International Version (NIV). Use any translation that you and your group feel comfortable with—it is sometimes interesting to compare different translations.

To prepare for a session you should:

• read through the main passage(s) for the session;

• read through the study notes and think about how you might approach the questions;

• think of the people in the group. How familiar are they with the passage and what might their questions be? Keep in mind that you are not so much looking for 'right' answers but are working through the possible meaning together;

• look up the leader's notes and note any materials you need;

• read through the Overview and Verse-by-verse notes. They will help you to understand more, and to grow in your own understanding;

• think about the aims of the study session and how they will work with your group;

• pray for your group members and for the group's time together.

There is a reading list at the back in case you want to look up things out of personal interest. It is not required reading!

# How do I lead a study group?

It may be that you have never led a small group Bible study before. Or you may be an old hand at it. Whatever your experience of small group Bible study may be, here are some hints and suggestions for leading your group through this particular material.

### Discussion and exploration...

First and foremost, small groups function best as discussion and exploration groups. They are not really a place where the leader—or anyone else—should expect to tell others what to believe or what to think. Of course, there will always be times when group members need to be guided and focused in their exploration. But, nevertheless, these are discussion and exploration groups, and certainly not the place for anyone to indulge themselves in sermons, diatribes or monologues. When discussion dries up and the discussion feels a little stilted, it can be very tempting for leaders to jump in and talk too much. In the long run, it is best to resist this temptation, compelling though it is. If conversation dies, it's not the end of the world—you can always move on to another point! Discussion points are indicated in the Study notes by the faces icon.

### Feeling safe to ask questions...

You should expect very little of the study material to admit of a direct or one-word answer. Small groups are places where people should feel free to speak their thoughts and their feelings and to open their hearts to others without being thought 'wrong' or 'unsound'. The questions are there to encourage discussion and exploration, not to provide pat 'answers'. People don't tend to grow by having their prejudices massaged and their assumptions confirmed!

### Guiding and encouraging discussion...

'How long should I let discussion run on?' There is a tension here. On the one hand, good discussion is valuable, and shouldn't be unduly stifled by the leader. If a particular part of the study seems to 'catch fire', or to raise interesting questions for the group, you may well need to stick with it and let discussion develop. Sometimes it is best simply to 'go with the flow'. On the other hand, it is a pity to let 'red herrings' take up the time, so that you only get part of the way through the material. These study notes are not just a clutch of questions, thrown together at random. They tend to have an inbuilt momentum. Quite often, the 'guts' of the study are to be found towards the end of the session, and need to be got to if members are to benefit fully from the material. You will need to think about timings. *In Jonah you will find there are key questions highlighted in bold italic in the study notes.* In Exodus, where the material is structured rather differently, there are no specific key questions. In Exodus there is more than enough material in each study notes for a session of an hour and a half. You will need carefully to assess beforehand which aspects you want particularly to concentrate on and select questions as necessary. In all this, do try to get to the end of the study. And don't forget the prayer and worship at the end of each of the sessions, which are an integral part of the material.

### The leader's role...

'So what is a leader's role?' Not to preach; not to provide 'the answers'; but to facilitate and encourage discussion and reflection. Some of these studies invite group members to offer thoughts and insights from their own life experiences. People can feel very vulnerable when they attempt this. So part of a leader's task is to help members feel secure enough to share appropriately in the life of the group.

### Worship and prayer...

'Should our group worship and pray together?' Ideally, yes. Some groups take to this more easily than others. This material is designed to engage the whole person, to warm the heart as well as to stimulate thinking. There will be opportunities for sharing, for prayer, for silent meditation. The studies may invite people to speak, to look and to taste. Do encourage members to participate in this; but do also be aware of your group members' individual needs and expectations. People have very different temperaments; they tend to come from rather different backgrounds and church traditions; and they often have very different experiences of discussion, prayer and worship. The secret is invariably: don't impose, rather encourage.

# Jonah: Reluctant prophet, merciful God

# 1 Introduction

To get you thinking about some of the themes of the book of Jonah, you are invited to play a game entitled...

---

**'Anything but *that*, Lord!'**

Deep down in our heart of hearts, there is a place (far or near!) where we are fervently hoping God will not call us to serve him, and a task or act of service (huge or tiny!) we are desperately hoping God will never call us to do. But how might you react if the worst happened...?

1      Take two small pieces of paper each.

2      Write on one the *place* or *kind of place*—here or abroad— where you hope God will never call you to go.

3      Write on the other the *task* or *kind of task* you hope God will never call you to do.

4      Put all the pieces of paper in a container.

5      Pull out one piece of paper at a time and try to guess who wrote it. You may learn something about each other!

(By the way: the purpose of this exercise is *not* to make you think that God might necessarily have called you in any of these ways!)

Then discuss some of the following questions together. Share insights arising out of some of the words you put down on the pieces of paper.

• What might there be about the *place* that might make you reluctant to go there?

• What might there be about the *task* that might make you dubious about doing it?

• What might there be about *yourself* and the *gifts* you think you have which might make you hesitate?

• What might there be about the *people* you might meet which might give you grounds for concern?

• What might there be about *God*, or your relationship with him, that might make you think long and hard about going to that place or doing that task?

• What sort of steps do you think you would take if you felt God was calling you to do this thing or go to this place?

Jonah was faced with an unexpected (and unwelcome!) commission. The book of Jonah explores his dealings with God as he reacted to God's call and came to terms with the purposes and acts of God. Nobody is suggesting that you are on the receiving end of an unwelcome commission from God—though you can never rule it out! But we can learn much about God and about ourselves from seeing how Jonah and God reacted to each other in this story...

_P.895

**Jonah 1:1–3**

# Call and flight

P.384

After our introductory exercise, we look at the first three verses only of the book of Jonah, just to whet your appetites!

Read the passage, then pool what you can find out about Jonah, Nineveh and Tarshish from a Bible map and from books in the Bible other than Jonah itself (read, for instance, 2 Kings 14:25; 2 Kings 19:35–37; Nahum 3:1–7; Psalm 72:10; Isaiah 66:18–19).

P.392 P.907 P.577 P.728

From what you have discovered, what sort of place would you imagine Nineveh to be? Why, in the story, might it be Nineveh that Jonah is told to go to?

Where, roughly, is Tarshish? What do you think Tarshish stands for in this story? *'spain (ends of earth as then known)*

Try to imagine that this is the first time you have heard the story of Jonah. After hearing these first three verses, what strikes you about Jonah that is different from other Old Testament prophets?

What considerations may have motivated Jonah's flight? What possibilities can you think of here? (Stick with the first three verses to answer this, for the purposes of this study.) Do we know yet exactly why he fled?

*Stage a debate, like this:*

• Half of the group are to side with God and try to argue for his demands on Jonah.

• Half of the group are to side with Jonah and try to justify his actions so far.

• Spend some time debating, in your two teams, who is in the right so far, Jonah or God? Stick to what we have read in these first three verses for this purpose.

*Afterwards, discuss together the following questions:*

• *How much sympathy do you feel for Jonah's position and his response so far? Why?*

• *To what extent do you feel, so far, God was justified in giving this commission to Jonah? Why?*

*• How much—or how little—information do we have to go on? What sorts of things haven't we been told? What gaps are there in our knowledge? Why might that be so?*

*• Ignoring, if you can, your previous knowledge of the rest of the book of Jonah, if you were God, what would you do next? Why?*

### Reflection and prayer

Sometimes God asks us to do things that seem extraordinary and perplexing, things that put us on the line. Sometimes God doesn't seem to want to give us all the information we think we need to complete the task. Sometimes the 'full picture' isn't made available to us at the outset.

Has this ever happened to you? How did you react? What was the outcome?

Read Psalm 55:1–8 together. How well does this express Jonah's predicament? How does it differ from how Jonah reacts?

Pray for people—including yourselves, as appropriate—who find immediate obedience to God's will difficult at times to carry out.

## GROWTH POINTS

# 2 Heathen sailors? Faithful servant? Wrathful God?

This time we look at the consequences of Jonah's disobedience, and we find God nevertheless at work through his actions. Read the passage and then work through the questions.

---

### The narrator's picture of the sailors

What are the sailors' responses to the storm (verse 5)?

What is the captain's approach (verse 6) to the question of prayer in times of danger? How might this conflict with what Jonah and the reader know?

Why do they respond as they do to Jonah's assertion of verse 9?

Why do you think they at first reject Jonah's request of verse 12?

What is the outcome (verses 15–16) as far as the sailors are concerned? Who and what has brought this about?

In what ways does their 'fear' of 1:16 differ from that of verses 5–6?

---

### The narrator's picture of Jonah

What, in verse 5, is Jonah doing as the sailors rush around? Why do you think Jonah acts in this way?

What, might Jonah's words in verse 9 tell us about his view of God and God's power?

Why might Jonah have made the request we find in verse 12? What possibilities can you think of here? What might his hopes and motives be?

How do you rate Jonah's actions and motives in comparison with those of the sailors?

How might the sailors' lives have turned out differently if Jonah had done what God said in the first place?

How (un)successful has Jonah's flight been so far? In what ways?

### The narrator's picture of God

How, at the beginning of this passage, does it look as if God might be acting? What might God be intending to do?

By the end of verse 16, what can we say about God's plans for Jonah after his refusal to go to Nineveh?

By the end of this passage, what have we discovered about God's intentions towards the sailors? How does he fulfil those intentions?

### What might the narrator be trying to say?

Look up Deuteronomy 21:8, Psalms 115:3 and 135:6, and compare this with what the sailors say. How well or badly do the sailors act, on the whole? And yet how would they have coped with the storm on their own? On the other hand, why should they have had to cope with it in the first place?

*What could this passage have to say to us about how God might relate to members of other faiths, and about what he might wish for them?*

*What could this passage have to say to us about how we should relate to them?*

How well or badly does Jonah act? Yet what would have happened if he had obeyed God in the first place? So far, what has been the effect of Jonah's actions: in implementing God's will, or in failing to do so?

*What might this passage have to say about the nature of God's calling and our obedience to it?*

*What might it say about God's sovereignty, and human free will?*

*How might it challenge us about our service to God? How might it encourage us?*

### Reflection and prayer

• Pray for our own understanding of how to relate to people of other faiths, and for our own testimony to the Lord Jesus Christ.

• Pray for any of other faiths (or of none) whom we know personally.

• Reflect on our own ways of fleeing from God.

**GROWTH POINTS**

## 3 Jonah 1:17—2:10
# A prayer from the belly of the fish

In this passage, we find Jonah down in the depths, in all sorts of ways. There he and God meet, perhaps for the first time, and we explore the relationship between them and God's demands on Jonah. Read the passage and then follow the questions through.

---

### Jonah's prayer

This prayer uses a lot of language about depth and distance. How many different sorts of ways of putting this can you find in this prayer?

Why is this language there? What does it convey about Jonah's position in this passage?

How has Jonah got into this position? What factors have operated to bring him here? Why is he here? For what purpose?

This passage implies that everything is within God's sight, hearing and control. What, then, about really bad things, real disasters, things that one would say are evil? How might we fit these things into our understanding of God?

How does Jonah respond to his plight? What is new about this for him? expressing feelings to God. a relationship.

Verse 8 speaks of the worship of vain idols. In his experience with the sailors, has Jonah learnt anything, and what? How quickly has Jonah learnt, in comparison with the sailors?

The Jonah of this passage seems a very different person to the Jonah of chapter 1. How big a change has taken place? How different is Jonah, deep down? How do you think he is likely to behave once he gets out of this scrape?

---

### Jonah's experience—our experience?

For this part of the study, it would be best, if numbers permit, to get into groups of two or three people. That will make it easier to be open. This part of the study asks you to consider sharing, with one or two others, experiences which may have been formative or even painful for you. *Do not feel obliged to offer anything you don't wish to talk about.* It is up to you to take responsibility for what you share.

How true to life are Jonah's behaviour and God's dealings with him?

Have there ever been times when we have been brought so low that we feel we could go no lower?

With the benefit of hindsight, how negative and how positive have those experiences turned out to be? Where might God be in them?

Jonah went through an experience of great desolation. Can experiences of desolation be used by God, and even be part of his will? Is that true of what we have experienced? In what way or ways?

In a time of great difficulty, we may say things of real significance to God. How easy is it for us to stand by those things? How different do things seem later, from another perspective, perhaps? How might we go about making these things stick?

## A response

In the same groups as you went into for discussion, take some time to pray about what you have discussed this evening. Pray through any issues that have arisen. Take the opportunity to pray for each other.

Why not have a go at writing a psalm-like prayer together, to help articulate some of the thoughts and feelings which have arisen for you as a result of this session? Each member could write a line or two of a 'psalm' separately, and you could then put them together, shuffling the lines around into some kind of order. Then you could read the 'psalm' out to the group.

## GROWTH POINTS

paper
pencils

pray at end.

# 4 Jonah 3:1–10

# Even the cattle repent!

As we have seen already, Jonah is a short book, yet it packs a huge amount of action and content into its four chapters. The author is able to do this partly because he has structured the book carefully. Here we pause briefly to appreciate some of the structure of the book.

The major 'characters' of chapter 1 were God, Jonah and the non-Israelite sailors. If we count the king and people of Nineveh as one 'character', there are also three major 'characters' in chapter 3.

In each of these chapters, God and Jonah play a role. Yet in each, we come across a different non-Israelite 'character'. But these non-Israelites, different though they are, react quite similarly to God's (and Jonah's) dealings with them. So chapters 1 and 3 are both concerned with a three-cornered relationship between God, Jonah and various non-Jewish people, and the themes of these chapters are built around those relationships.

In chapter 3, then, we meet some more foreigners—as Jonah does. We discover for the first time what his message is to be—as he does. And the reactions to his message are perhaps not what he—or we—expected! Read the passage, and look at the questions which follow.

## God and Jonah (3:1–3)

In the Hebrew, there are similarities and contrasts aplenty between 1:1–3 and 3:1–3:

• In 1:1 the word of the Lord came to Jonah, and in 3:1 it comes to him a second time.

• In 1:2 and 3:2, Jonah is told, each time, to 'get up and go to Nineveh, that great city...' In 1:1 he was told to cry out against it. But in 3:1 he is told to proclaim a message to it.

• In 1:3, Jonah got up... and fled. In 3:3, Jonah also gets up... but this time he obeys.

What might these similarities and contrasts suggest to us about *God*, about his purposes, and about his call to his servants?

What might they suggest to us about *Jonah*, about his attitude towards God, and about his part in God's plans?

What might they suggest to us about *Nineveh*, about what it represented, and about the likely outcome of Jonah's mission? *will succeed?*

*God knows he will succeed*

## God, Jonah and the people of Nineveh (3:4–10)

There is lots of calling and crying out and proclaiming in the book of Jonah! This cluster of words provides us with some more similarities and contrasts between chapters 1 and 3. Let's look at them:

• What had Jonah been told to do in 1:2? And how did he respond then?

• What had the captain told him to do in 1:6, and how had he responded?

• What is Jonah now told to do when he gets to Nineveh (3:2)? And what does he do now in consequence (3:4)?

• What might these things tell us about Jonah and of his development?

• What were the results (in 1:14) of Jonah's disobedience? What, now, are the results (in 3:5 and 3:8) of his new-found obedience?

• What might this tell us of the sailors and of the Ninevites, and of their responsiveness to God? And about God and how he uses Jonah?

Discuss Jonah's message in 3:4. What kind of message is it? What might it suggest to us about the nature and activity of God amongst human beings?

Consider 3:7–10. What gives rise to God's forgiveness? The Ninevites' repentance? The sovereign will of God? How might these things fit together?

## Implications: the place of mission    *— A community?*

Review together the place where you live and worship, and the place where you work, and particularly the people who make up that community or those communities. As objectively as you can, ask the following questions:

• What groups of people live and work in our community, broadly speaking? *groups.*

*retired people*
*school children*
*youths/teenagers*
*mothers/babies*
*middle class/streets*
*working/unemployed/*
*low paid*

*teenagers ✗ □*
*middle class*
*good life*
*'style' god ✗ etc*

- Which people or groups of people do we find most resistant to the gospel? Why? What does this say about them, their preoccupations and their cultural setting?

- Which people or groups of people do we find most open to the gospel? Why? What does this say about them? *younger children* *people we have* *Befriended,*

- How does this passage from Jonah affect the way you see these people and the possibility of their believing and trusting in God? *— sowing 'seeds'*

## Implications: the practice of mission

Assess together your mission, as individuals and as a church, to the community in which you live and worship, and/or that in which you work. Consider the following:

- In which areas and with which groups of people have we been least effective? Why? *teenagers – church offers little*

- Which groups of people do we find we have been hesitant or reluctant to engage with? Why?

- In which areas and with which groups of people have we been more effective? Why?

- What does all this suggest about our church, our preoccupations and our church culture?

- How does this passage from Jonah affect the way you see your mission and its effectiveness? What lessons or insights would you draw for the future mission of your church?

## Finally... *Sing First*

Spend some time praying for the community you live and worship in, and/or the one you work in. Pray for yourselves as a church and a home group, in the light of your discussions.

**GROWTH POINTS**

151 – for i'm building a people
of power

626 Teach me thy way

# 5 Jonah 4:1–11 P.897
# Moaning at a merciful God

Again, we pause briefly to notice something else about the structure of the book of Jonah. In chapter 2, we met two major 'characters'—Jonah and, indirectly, God. In chapter 4, we again meet these two 'characters', and only them. Again, the action centres around these characters. So chapters 2 and 4 both centre around the relationship between God and Jonah, a relationship which has been worked out through their dealings with the sailors (in chapter 1) and the Ninevites (in chapter 3). And so we now turn to chapter 4.

---

### Summary

Before you read the passage, briefly summarize the story so far. Concentrate on these three questions:

- In what ways has Jonah acted?

- Why might he have acted in these ways?

- How much have we been told about his motives so far?

---

### Jonah takes it badly that bad behaviour doesn't lead to a bad end! (Jonah 4:1–4)

How have the Ninevites reacted to Jonah's message? How has God reacted to the Ninevites' reaction? How does Jonah react in verse 1 to God's reaction to the Ninevites' reaction?

The wordplay of the last question was deliberate—if clumsy! The original Hebrew puts the diverse reactions of the Ninevites, God and Jonah together by a wordplay.

Try a wordplay of your own in English: the Ninevites re _ _ nted; God re _ _ nted; Jonah re _ _ nted!

On the basis of verse 1, what is this chapter likely to be about?

1 repented
2 relented
3 resented

### A surprise in store for the reader! (Jonah 4:2–5)

Verse 2 is a surprise to us! Why do you think the narrator has left it so late to tell us this? How does it affect our understanding of Jonah and his motives? Why—on the face of it—has he been resisting God?

Follow Jonah's statement about God in verse 2 through the pages of the OT (any of Psalms 86:15; 103:8; 145:8; Exodus 34:6; Nehemiah 9:17, 31; Joel 2:13 will help here). What do you make of this confession on Jonah's lips? Should we take it at face value? What might be going on behind these words in Jonah's mind?

Jonah's request to die has a good pedigree in the OT. It reminds us of Elijah in 1 Kings 19:4 and of Israel in Exodus 14:12. What *persecution* prompted *them* to make this request? What prompts *Jonah*? What might this tell us about Jonah? *an expected attack by Pharaoh*

What does God ask Jonah? What is Jonah's response?

### On the receiving end of a gentle lesson (Jonah 4:6–11)

So far, what do we think is on Jonah's mind? Why is he reacting as he is?

What is the purpose of the bush? What is Jonah's reaction to it? What does this suggest to us about his thoughts and intentions?

When the bush withers, Jonah repeats his request of verse 3. What does this suggest to us?

In response, God asks another question. How similar is it, and how different, to the question in verse 4? What does God think of Jonah's actions?

Jonah is caught in a dilemma. Explore together his possible answers and their implications. What if he answers 'yes'? What if he answers 'no'?

What is the purpose of God's lesson to Jonah in verses 10 and 11?

### Some implications for us

In what specific areas of our individual and communal lives do we think like Jonah?

How willing are we to admit to these thoughts? In what specific ways do we put these thoughts behind a smoke-screen? What kinds of smoke-screens do we use?

Share an aspect of your Christian beliefs where you are at your most convinced, inflexible and dogmatic! Here are some examples:

• 'A service isn't a service without choruses.'

• 'It is impossible, or at least difficult, for liberal Christians to have a real faith.'

• 'Evangelical Christians are simplistic and dogmatic in their faith.'

• 'God can't save you unless you've prayed a certain prayer.'

• 'Baptism is only for adults, and for children of parents we are *certain* are believers.'

• 'A service isn't a service without an organ and a choir.'

• 'God doesn't heal people today.'

But do think of your own!

To what extent is your most treasured belief held because of its truth, and to what extent is it there to protect you from uncertainty and the threat of change?

How might you react if this belief were challenged? What if God were to ask you to allow this belief to be developed, stretched or expanded?

---

### A response to the book of Jonah

• Stage a dramatic reading of the whole of the book of Jonah. There are various ways of doing this. One reader could act as narrator, another as God, another as Jonah, and so on. Or someone could read out the story while other group members act or mime out the action.

• What three new insights do you, as a group, want to take away with you from your study of Jonah?

• How, specifically, are you going to allow those things to make a difference in your lives?

• Offer these things—and anything else on your minds—to God in prayer.

242 Hosanna
388 Jesus we enthrone you.

# Introduction

## Why study Jonah?

Here are some brief reasons for studying Jonah:

• The book of Jonah is many things at once: an exciting story and yet also a sophisticated piece of theological writing; a good yarn and yet also a complex and many-faceted work of art. It has much to offer us. It's a book all can both enjoy and benefit from.

• The book of Jonah is short: it can be studied—at some depth—as a whole book from beginning to end within five study sessions.

• One main theme of Jonah is that of *mission*, in its widest sense. What are God's intentions towards the people of the world? What is the believer's role in those purposes?

• Another theme in Jonah is that of *calling* and response to calling. There is plenty of room in our churches for more people to be using their gifts in ministry and service. Studying Jonah will encourage and challenge people in this area. It gives us room to ask: What am *I* called to do? How do *I* respond?

• There is another issue in Jonah as well: *What is God like?* How does he act? How predictable or comprehensible is he? Is he essentially wrathful

or forgiving? Or both? Which comes first? How do these sides of God fit together? This should be a fruitful area for discussion in groups.

## Date and authorship

The Jonah, son of Amittai, mentioned in 2 Kings 14:25 is unlikely to be the author of the book of Jonah, simply because it is probably a later work than the eighth century BC, when the historical Jonah lived. In fact, we do not know for sure who wrote this book, or what his background was. For the relationship between the historical Jonah and the Jonah portrayed in this book, see the leader's notes to the first session.

Scholars date the book of Jonah around the fifth to fourth centuries BC, well after the end of the exile in Babylon between 587 and 539BC. Various aspects of the text suggest this, including late vocabulary, certain aspects of its style. Sometimes the dating of a book may assist in appreciating its theology: a knowledge of the context out of which it was written can often be a great help towards understanding it. But that is less true of Jonah, for any recons- truction of this period of Israel's history seems itself fairly tentative.

## The structure of Jonah

The book of Jonah has been very carefully structured, and this is apparent in all sorts of ways. There are a number of different symmetries or balances to the book.

• It falls into two distinct parts, 1:1 to 2:10; and 3:1 to 4:11.

• Each of those parts is started by sections which parallel each other: 1:1–3, where God tells Jonah to 'get up' and do something, and he heads off in the other direction; and 3:1–4, where God again tells Jonah to 'get up', and this time he obeys.

• Each of these two sections can be broken down into two sub-sections. A = 1:1 to 1:16. B = 1:17 to 2:10. C = 3:1 to 3:10. D = 4:1 to 4:11. Each sub-section roughly follows the chapter divisions, thus:

Section 1: *1:1—2:10*
    **A** *1:1–16*
        **B** *1:17—2:10*
Section 2: *3:1—4:11*
    **C** *3:1–10*
        **D** *4:1–11*

• Sub-sections A and C are in parallel, as are B and D.

• A and C involve Jonah, God and non-Israelites (in A, the sailors; in C the Ninevites). In each case, the non-Israelites are put through a difficult set of circumstances (a storm; Jonah's message), yet their situation is resolved favourably (the sailors are brought to worship God; the Ninevites are brought to repentance). Not so with Jonah, who is also put through it, but who in A is thrown into the sea and whose role in C as harbinger of doom brings about a repentance which God seems happy to accept!

• B and D involve just Jonah and God. So the agenda of those chapters is different, concerning more the relationship between Jonah and God and questions about Jonah's call and the effects of God's call upon his servant.

• These parallels allow the narrator to deal carefully in comparisons and contrasts between Jonah and the 'heathens', Jonah and God, the 'heathens' and God, and so on. Some of this will be brought out later in the studies.

• There are further parallelisms and structural symmetries within some of the sub-sections. These will be explained as necessary. Some of this will be mentioned at the beginning of the fourth and fifth sessions (see the study notes).

## What kind of book is Jonah?

Jonah is to be found, in the English and Hebrew Bibles, among the Twelve Prophets. And yet a look at Jonah will show that it is most unlike the other eleven of those books. The other books are collections of prophecies. Jonah is not: it contains only five direct words of prophecy in the Hebrew (3:5). The book is about a prophet; but it is not a prophetic book in the sense that the others are.

So what kind of book is Jonah? This is in itself a difficult question. There is certainly still plenty of scholarly debate about the kind of book Jonah is and what its purpose and meaning are. The book has been interpreted as an allegory—similar to *Pilgrim's Progress*—but this is far from convincing. Some have seen its meaning as comprehensively defined by the Gospel writers' use of the book on the lips of Jesus (Matthew 12:39–41, 16:4; Luke 11:29–32), but this hardly allows the book of Jonah to speak on its own terms.

Some statements can be made relatively safely. For one, Jonah is probably not meant as history-writing: it doesn't set out to give a historically accurate account of the life or activities of the prophet Jonah. This is an important point. We can get hung up on the question of the book's *historicity*: 'Did what is recorded actually happen?' The important issue is not so much whether the events related in the book actually took place, but rather what kind of writing the book contains. It is rather like *Macbeth*: issues about historical accuracy might conceivably arise over the account in Holinshed's *Chronicles*, from which Shakespeare drew his plot; but one wouldn't ask the same questions of Shakespeare's play, simply because it does not profess to be history-writing. The *status* of the book of Jonah as scripture does not depend on the *historical accuracy* of its contents. So questions about its historical accuracy should be put on the back burner for the purposes of these studies!

What sort of writing is Jonah then, if not history-writing? Scholars differ still. These are some of the questions scholars ask: Is it right to look for a single meaning to the book, or does deliberate ambiguity lie at its heart? Are we to laugh at Jonah or to sympathize with him in his unpalatable task? What kind of audience was the book originally addressed to? Is the book about the prophetic calling; about mission; about encouragement over the possibility of repentance; about the tension between the compassion and judgment of God; or about any number of these issues?

Any judgment we arrive at as to the type of book it is and as to what it may mean is bound to have its detractors. The scholar H.W. Wolff persuasively describes the book as (first of all) a *short story* which (secondly) *teaches* its readers or hearers something about God, his servants and the peoples of the world (thirdly) by means of *irony*.

To expand on that a little. First, the book can be seen as a short story.

Secondly, the narrator treats, by means of a story, a number of issues of belief relevant to the situation of his readers. Themes of 'fear', 'repentance', 'pity', and 'evil' pervade the book. The teaching nature of the book can particularly be seen in its final open question. The book is aimed at those who cannot understand God's forbearance with foreign peoples who have harassed Israel for many years. Are they to be judged or forgiven? It is aimed at those who are too bound up in gloomy concern with themselves to trouble about 'outsiders'. It is aimed at those who have forgotten the free nature of God's pity.

Thirdly, the *strategy* by which this purpose is carried through is *irony*. But, if there is irony in this book, who is the target? Probably the irony is directed against Jonah himself.

Scholars variously see the portrait of Jonah in the book as a 'caricature', which shows him up as 'mean' and even perhaps 'malevolent'. But the evidence is not all one way. For instance, what of Jonah's prayer in chapter 2? Is it an honest expression of contrition? If so, how does it square with Jonah's later waywardness? Or is it meant to be read as an inadequate or shallow expression of willingness to obey God?

Some scholars do not agree that Jonah is the target of character assassination by irony. Some see him as a *comic hero*. In that case, God becomes an inscrutable, even frightening figure, at times peremptory, at times sympathetic and patient. Even if this is true of how God is described, it seems unlikely that Jonah is meant to be seen as a comic hero. He is certainly often described in a pointed and fairly unsympathetic way, even if not in quite such stark terms as some commentators suggest.

Whatever one's views here, the issue seems to be this: there is a sparring match—with a serious purpose—portrayed in this book between God and Jonah. Both cannot be right all of the time! Either Jonah is the wayward one and God the rightful corrector of his misdeeds; or Jonah is the (relatively) innocent victim of God's unpredictable actions. Views differ. We may well see that the balance between these characters changes as the story develops. At times Jonah seems plain wrong; at times, though, God does seem fairly inscrutable!

One final insight. The commentator Fretheim sees the central point of the book as being the issue of God's compassion and justice, the age-old question: 'How can God be just without compromising his mercy, and compassionate without compromising his justice?' Fretheim argues that the book of Jonah makes clear that 'God is not programmed to respond in fixed ways to certain patterns of human behaviour'. God has divine compassion and sovereign freedom. God may destroy (3:4) and he may save (3:9). In this sense, the 'who knows' (NRSV) of 3:9 is justified. The fact that Jonah is called to be a prophet does not mean that he has an inside knowledge of God's ultimate purposes.

Because it seems amenable to very different interpretations, the book of Jonah can be maddening! But the same quality also means it can be most rewarding. In fact, it seems almost as many-sided as the God to whom it witnesses! The best we can say here is that many of these themes will surface as we go along, with different slants and emphases. Perhaps we should not be too ready to pigeonhole the book of Jonah. Maybe we should also draw back from utterly condemning or overly applauding Jonah himself; and from either taping down the God it portrays or from thinking him totally unpredictable and contrary. If we go to any of these extremes, the narrator is likely to have the last laugh on us!

# 1 Jonah 1:1–3
# Call and flight

## Aims

• To get people thinking about the nature of God's calling and the range of human responses to it.

• To introduce people to the 'action' which takes place between Jonah and God in the book of Jonah.

• To help people appreciate the ambiguities, gaps and questions we are left with by the end of verse 3.

• To whet people's appetite for the next session!

NB: The introductory session and the first study have been carefully constructed to dovetail into each other. The first study will work best if preceded by the introductory exercise.

## Overview

These first three verses of Jonah are a small masterpiece of *compression*, *open-endedness* and *highlighting*.

*Compression*: first, in the form of the verses. They open with 'the word of the Lord'; and close with the repeated 'away from the presence of the Lord'. This bracketing knits these verses tightly together and puts God at the beginning and the end of the passage. Secondly, in the content: within just three verses we are introduced to the main characters; Jonah receives his prophetic commission; and he refuses it, leaving in the opposite direction.

*Open-endedness*: for all the speed with which the story moves, there are some great and deliberate gaps left in our understanding. We don't yet know the full nature of Jonah's message to Nineveh. We don't—as yet—know why he has refused God. And—above all—we don't know yet what God is going to do next.

There is also some careful *highlighting* going on. Nineveh stands for the big wicked Assyrian capital city; and that's probably as much as we are meant to know about it. Tarshish stands for the ends of the earth; again, that is probably all we are meant to know. This putting of historical and geographical detail well into the background leaves the foreground available for the main concern of this passage and of the whole story: the relationship between the main characters, God and Jonah. Wolff writes (page 103): 'The tension between [the Lord] and Jonah emerges as the main theme [of the book]; but the motifs that drive it forward are to be found in the relationship to Nineveh, and to the ship's crew as well.'

In this sense the story is meant to have a universal purpose. We are not meant to be too bothered about how historical the events are. The narrator's aim is to draw out some lessons about God and his people by means of an entertaining story.

So these verses introduce and *set up* the story, pushing history to the background, leaving the foreground for the action between God and his reluctant prophet. They also leave us with tensions and uncertainties which the rest of Jonah addresses. This gives rise, in the reader, to anticipation and a desire to know what is likely to happen next. This is just a taster for the rest of the book. Group members are supposed to leave with their appetites whetted for the next session!

## Verse-by-verse

1 '... the word of the Lord came...': a standard expression for God's revelation to a prophet, intended to evoke texts such as 1 Kings 17:8 and Jeremiah 1:4. The text remains silent as to how this word took place. The narrator points us more to the *fact* of the commission, rather than to the detail of its *content*.

Jonah-ben-Amittai is referred to at 2 Kings 14:25. There Jonah is recorded as prophesying to Jeroboam II, king of Israel 784–753BC. What is the link between this prophet and our Jonah? The book of Jonah is not primarily a history or a chronicle, but a story. As it was probably written much later than the eighth century BC, the links between the Jonah of 2 Kings and our Jonah are not supposed to be historically very strong. Why, then, choose Jonah as the main character of this story?

Wolff (page 98) argues as follows. The historical Jonah of 2 Kings had prophesied, correctly, that Israel's ancient frontiers would be restored despite its disobedience. Thus: salvation for Israel. This came about by battle. Thus: judgment for Israel's enemies. At the time Assyria (capital: Nineveh) was Israel's main enemy. So the historical Jonah is a prophet of salvation for Israel and a prophet of judgment for Israel's enemy Assyria. To choose Jonah as the main character strengthens the idea that God intends destruction against Nineveh. The original audience would have known that Assyria was to be the destroyer of the historical Jonah's northern homeland. As a result, the

turnaround in 3:6, 10, where Nineveh repents and God turns from destruction, comes all the more as a surprise.

2 'Go...': NIV misses the point here. The Hebrew reads: '*Arise*, go to Nineveh...'; and in verse 3 Jonah '*arose*... to flee'! The repetition of the verb 'arise' sets up a contrast between the command and Jonah's action.

'The great city' often applied to Nineveh here. Nineveh was destroyed in 612BC, long before Jonah was written. Wolff (page 99): 'Nineveh has been stripped of every historical feature'. The narrator is not interested in the detail of Nineveh; not in the fact that it was an improbable distance on foot from Israel, nor in the fact that it wasn't the capital of Assyria at the time of the historical Jonah. He gives it a greater size than it reasonably can have had. So he doesn't seem interested in Nineveh for itself, but rather as an *archetype* and universal example of a great, wicked city.

'Preach against it': we are not told what Jonah is to say; and we are probably meant to think that Jonah hasn't been told at this stage either!

Is Jonah to proclaim Nineveh's doom, with no opportunity to repent? Or is repentance a possibility inherent within the declamation by Jonah of God's message? The former seems more likely, for reasons given above.

'Wickedness': the Hebrew *ra'ah* is often used in this book. It is capable of a wide range of meanings, and that shading is used effectively in Jonah. Here it means wicked acts and attitudes. In 3:8, 10, 'wicked ways' extends this notion, implying a settled course of life. In 1:7–8, it is used in terms of human calamity. In 3:10 it refers to God's divine punishment. In 4:1,6, it is used in a weaker sense, implying human 'displeasure' or 'discomfort'.

3 Jonah doesn't even stop to argue! There are precedents for protesting at God's command: Exodus 4:10; Jeremiah 1:6; but Jonah doesn't even hang around for that! This sets up great suspense for the reader—for the normal

reaction to God's 'Go!' is 'he went'.

Note that we are given no reason for Jonah's fleeing. This comes later in the book—as something of a surprise!—but for now we are deliberately left guessing. It is significant for a proper reading of this book that we do not cut across the grain of the narrative by importing the resolution (or complication!) of this issue in 4:2 into this earlier part of the story. We are not supposed to know at this stage what is on Jonah's mind!

'Tarshish—away from the Lord': Tarshish may be modern Baetis, in south-western Spain, beyond the Pillars of Hercules and thus beyond the known world of the time. It is also in the opposite direction to Nineveh. Jonah is going as far away as he can to escape God; but in vain, as he later admits in 1:9.

'He went down to Joppa...': first, we have a literary technique involving the verb *yarad*, to descend. Jonah makes a literal descent: *down* to Joppa; *down* into the ship (1:3: NIV, 'went aboard'); *down* into the bowels of the ship in 1:5 as the storm breaks; *down* to the roots of the mountains in 2:6. The text implies that Jonah makes a figurative, *spiritual* descent also, into the depths of despair and disobedience, whilst the sailors, in contrast, move closer to God through the experience of the storm.

Another technique here is that 'he went down' is the first of five verbs—found, bound for/going to, paid, went down/boarded—which rush headlong over each other and give us the sense of haste. Jonah, here, is rather comic in his haste.

The Hebrews distrusted the sea. The fact that Jonah was willing to board ship to get away will have emphasized his determination to the original hearers.

'Away from the Lord': repeated from earlier in the verse. This provides a small link between the beginning of the book ('The word of the Lord came...') and the end of this section ('... away from the Lord'), stressing the contrast between God's command and Jonah's reaction. So, as Jonah heads for Tarshish, he moves away and downwards.

*[margin: Spain]*

## 2 Jonah 1:4–16
# Heathen sailors? Faithful servant? Wrathful God?

## Aims

• To enjoy the way this story is written!

• To explore the actions and motivations of the sailors, of Jonah and of God as the narrator depicts them.

• To ask questions about the way God uses his servants, and about the related issue of cooperation and free will.

• To ask questions about how God relates to those 'outside the covenant', and about how we should relate to them too.

## Overview

This study is written in such a way that the more *textual* questions in the first three sections lead up to the more *general* questions of the last section. That last section is perhaps the most worthwhile part of the study.

There is considerable artistry in the writing of this passage:

1. As Wolff (page 108) points out, there is strong linkage between its beginning (1:4–5) and its end (1:15–16). This linkage is evident in the use of three word-clusters: (1)

fear; (2) God/gods; and (3) the sea. This linkage involves both similarity (the same words) and change (development in the story).

*Beginning (1:4–5)*         *End (1:15–16)*
*1:4 God sends the storm over the sea*
                    *1:15 The sea calms down*
*1:5 The sailors are afraid and cry to their gods*
                    *1:16 They fear God greatly*

So great change occurs in the sea and in the sailors. What brings it about? Most directly, Jonah. In the central section (particularly 1:9, the nucleus of this passage) Jonah is presented as the direct reason for these changes. And in 1:9 we find these same word-clusters re-occurring: 'I am a Hebrew and I *fear* Yahweh, the *God* of heaven, who made the *sea* and the dry land'.

2. Of course, the same word may not signify the same thing every time it is used. Not only does the word 'fear' link the problem (the sailors' fear) with the outcome (their fear of God) through Jonah ('I fear the Lord'), as explained above. It also reflects the different states of mind of the people to which it is applied. The sailors are afraid because of the storm (1:5). Jonah's fear (1:9) of the Lord is merely a conventional statement of religious adherence, and not a true expression of obedient faith. The sailors' response, nevertheless, is one of even starker fear (1:10): literally, they 'feared a great fear'. And, *paradoxically*, Jonah's assertion in 1:9 and his suggestion in 1:12 give rise to the lulling of the storm and the sailors' great fear of the Lord (1:16)!

3. There is another catchword linking the beginning of the passage with its central section and its end: the word for 'to throw'. It occurs in 1:4, where Yahweh *throws* the storm onto the sea (NIV misses this completely); in 1:5, where the sailors *throw* cargo overboard to save the ship; and in 1:12 and 15 it is only when, at Jonah's suggestion, they *throw* him into the sea that they are saved and come to fear God.

4. The fourth example occurs at 1:15. Until that point, Jonah and the sailors are together on the boat, but at 1:15 their ways separate. Thereafter, we find a short passage (1:16) which happily resolves the position of the sailors. Not so with Jonah. He is in the sea! God's dealings with him are by no means over, and we are still left wondering what is going to happen to him.

These four examples of narrative art are not there just for fun: they take their place in the narrator's wider strategy, which is that of *irony*. Jonah sleeps—the sailors exert themselves. Jonah coolly acknowledges God, and carries on running—the crew tries hard to do God's will. Jonah refuses to take a message to the many Ninevites—the sailors try hard to save their one passenger. Yet it is Jonah who, despite himself, is the key to the (physical and spiritual) rescue of the sailors!

This irony is not employed for its own sake either: it is there for a

33

teaching purpose. Wolff is worth quoting more fully (pages 109, 123): 'How the narrator laughs at a Hebrew who takes great pains to flee from his God, and in the very process, and quite against his will, brings non-Israelites to believe in this God!... Through the medium of satiric narrative, our storyteller teaches that the God of Jonah, the Hebrew, is able to find among completely strange people the obedience and trust which his own messenger denied him.' And yet, although that is true, God is so sovereign that he can use even a fleeing recalcitrant for his purposes. Jonah cannot escape his calling—and nor can any of God's people. Wolff (page 123): 'The heathen are undoubtedly more humane, more active, wiser, and also more devout. And Jonah is undoubtedly exposed to ridicule. And yet it is only he who can tell the others how they have to behave'.

The sailors are sympathetically depicted in this story. And yet they still need God's prophet, recalcitrant and awkward though he is, to bring them to the worship of Jonah's God. Perhaps this chapter subtly points us towards a proper approach towards those of other faiths. On the one hand, we should extend every respect towards them, recognizing their search for God to be genuine and sincere. We should try sincerely and honestly to understand other faiths at their very best. On the other hand, we should expect that, like Jonah, we have a role to play, as we relate to those of other faiths, in bringing the God of Israel and of Jesus Christ before them, and in courteously commending him to them.

---

## Verse-by-verse

4 'But Yahweh...': Both of these words are emphatic in the Hebrew. The narrator stresses the fact that this storm is God's stark response to Jonah's flight. We have a new scene: the boat; and new actors: the sailors. But the links with the first three verses are clear.

'... Yahweh *threw* a great wind...': this acknowledges the use of the word 'throw' in verses 4, 5, 12 and 15: see notes, above.

5 Jonah has found his way to the lowest part of the ship. The use of the verb 'to descend' has already been noted in the first session's leader's notes: it is part of a process of spiritual descent in Jonah (1:3—used twice; 1:5; 2:6). Also, the phrase 'had gone down to the lowest part...' may hint at the common phrase 'going down to the pit', or 'the grave': e.g. Psalm 22:29. The more so since the psalm in Jonah 2 reprises this language (2:6).

There is irony here: the seamen are in a mad panic of activity, but achieve nothing. Jonah, on the other hand, sleeps through it all. One might expect God to honour their bustle, for it contrasts favourably with Jonah's lethargy. But not so! Even though Jonah is the one who has put everyone in danger, it seems that he is the only one who can get them out of it! And he does—but rather despite himself.

6 'Get up and call...': the narrator pokes fun here. These are the very words which God spoke to Jonah at the outset of his adventure.

8 The sailors' detailed enquiries of Jonah seem a little out of place in a life-endangering storm. However, this does hint that these non-Israelite sailors are 'anything but examples of heedless violence' (Wolff, page 114). Jonah skirts

34

around their question 'what do you do?', and only answers their last enquiry.

9 'Worship': so NIV. More literally 'fear', little more than an acknowledgment of his religious affiliation. His religion seems rather wan and conventional compared to that of the sailors later, just as his lethargy has contrasted badly with their activity.

'The Lord': in an emphatic position here in the Hebrew. Jonah explains who Yahweh is: the one true God, who has sovereignty over all he has created.

12 Is Jonah's suggestion an indication of his desire to obey God, or of his obstinacy? At least his admission of guilt is a step forward for him. But there is no prayer or confession from him; his desire seems to be for a escape by death; in comparison with the sailors he remains intractable.

13 The satirical view of Jonah is confirmed by the sailors' reaction. They generously try other approaches first. But their attempts fail.

14 Yet still they do not do as Jonah wishes. Instead, they pray—the longest piece of speech in the passage. They, non-Israelite sailors, plead with Yahweh, not Jonah, as far as we know, as he was asked to do in 1:6. The verb used is that same one ('to call') that Yahweh uses when asking Jonah to preach against Nineveh. Golka (page 86): 'It would appear that the pagans are rather better at it!'

To show how correctly they are acting, the narrator even puts traditional Israelite phrases into their mouths: Deuteronomy 21:8. And the final phrase of their speech mirrors the Israelite psalmic words: Psalms 115:3; 135:6. Here are foreign sailors acting as model Israelites. A contrast to the actions of Jonah himself!

16 The men act as those with new faith in Yahweh.

# 3 Jonah 1:17—2:10
# A prayer from the belly of the fish

---

## Aims

• To examine something of the stylistic means the poetry of this passage uses to achieve its aims.

• To consider how Jonah's prayer—and what it tells us of Jonah—may fit into the rest of the book.

• To encourage members to reflect on, and to share appropriately, how Jonah's experience relates to their experiences of life and of God.

---

## Overview

Here we have a *self-contained* scene of the book with a *poetic*, psalm-like prayer at its centre:
• The prayer itself is very different to anything else in the book. This is partly because of its *poetic* character.

• The whole scene is very *self-contained*. The events with the foreign sailors have been brought to a happy conclusion. And Jonah has not yet got to Nineveh. So this is a sort of *interlude*. After all the noise and frenetic activity of the storm, and before the busyness of Jonah's arrival at Nineveh, all is quiet. And, in that quietness, Jonah communes alone with God.

This quiet, set-apart scene involves

just two actors: directly, Jonah, and indirectly, God, who has silently got Jonah into the fish and whom Jonah addresses.

There are links between chapter 2 and 1:1–3. The present passage is both similar to 1:1–3, and different from it. Similar, in that, as in 1:1–3, the interplay is just between Jonah and God. Different, in that a lot of water has flowed under the bridge (under the boat?) since then! The Jonah we first met is not entirely the Jonah we meet now; indeed, he is not exactly the same Jonah whom we shall meet later. In fact, the Jonah of chapter 2 seems a very different character, dramatically speaking, to the Jonah of the rest of the book.

For some interpreters, this *apparent tension* between the character of Jonah in chapter 2 and that in the rest of the book has proved a source of difficulty.

## The dramatic character of Jonah

The Jonah depicted in chapter 2 appears to be a repentant man who expresses his praise and gratitude to Yahweh out of a situation of deep despair. Yet this portrayal appears light years away from the cross-grained, hasty, sulky individual of the rest of the book! *Why the difference?*

Scholars adopt at least two broad lines of reasoning for this apparent contrast in the character of Jonah in this passage and his character in the rest of the book:

• At this point, as nowhere else, Jonah becomes a model for faith, and the psalm becomes a model prayer. But this does not explain why our model Jonah still seems to revert to type later.

• The psalm is an ironic comment upon Jonah himself. Its language is quite deliberately traditional, reflecting the Psalms. The narrator wants to depict a Jonah who 'uses pious language out of concern for himself, but has not one word of regret about his failure to carry out his mission to Nineveh' (Golka, page 93). According to this reading, then, Jonah's contrition is not meant to be taken at face value. This approach isn't very satisfying either. To have Jonah utter something sounding like a traditional psalm is surely a clumsy way of satirizing him.

Perhaps there is another solution. Far from being a 'psychologically unconvincing' portrayal of a reluctant prophet, the narrative depicts something true to human nature. The cross-grained Jonah becomes repentant enough—and he means it too!—when in a horrible fix. But all too quickly he reverts to his former behaviour once he has been rescued. Perhaps this account of Jonah is simply wise in its realism.

There is *paradox* in all this. Jonah has been descending so far. He has now reached the lowest point he can get to. He is surrounded by water, in the depths of the oceans and in the belly of the fish. He is all but lost. And yet it is here, in the depths, at the point of lostness, that he finds God and prays to him. This is the first time in the book that we find Jonah addressing God. Until now he has been fleeing. Now he stops and speaks. To be sure, there will be more anger, frustration, misunderstanding and rebellion ahead. And, in fact, the 'psalm' itself hints at this: see comments to verses 2, 8 and 9. But, for the moment at least, Jonah stops, turns to God, and speaks to him. And that can only be an improvement on his previous activity.

## The 'sign of Jonah'

This 'sign of Jonah' is mentioned three times in the Gospels, on the lips of Jesus: Matthew 12:39f, 16:4 and Luke 11:29.

Two things can be said about the interrelation between those texts and the book of Jonah.

First, negatively: although Jesus' reported use of the book of Jonah must be of great significance to Christians, we should not say that it exhaustively defines the meaning and significance of this OT book:

• The 'sign' only relates to the time Jonah spent in the fish, and ignores the rest of the book.

• If we were to see the prophet Jonah purely as a 'type' of Christ, then the significance of the book must have been totally obscure for any pre-Christian Jewish reader.

This sort of interpretation, which is of course valid in New Testament terms, views the book solely through the lens of the NT and risks failing to interpret it on its own terms. And interpreting the book of Jonah on its own terms is primarily what we are about in these studies.

Secondly, positively: Allen (page 196): 'Essentially Jesus referred to Jonah and the fish as a means of communicating the significance of his own mission. His fundamental concern was not to expound the book of Jonah but to reveal truth concerning himself in terms which his Jewish audience acknowledged and could understand... He turned to good use the current interpretation of Jonah 2 and made it the vehicle of vital truth.'

## Verse-by-verse

17 God appoints the fish—not necessarily a whale!—just as he will appoint a plant later in 4:6. According to the book of Jonah, Yahweh is the lord of nature and of creation.

There is dramatic *tension* here. On the one hand, the implication at the outset of this passage must surely be that Jonah is about to die. It is only when we read the 'psalm' and finally get to 2:10 that we realise that the fish is, after all, an agent of God's mercy and determination to use Jonah. On the other hand, we do have a hint as early as 1:17 that things may not be terminal for Jonah: we are told he was in the fish for a set period of time. All this increases the pressure: *What is going to happen to Jonah?*

1 A favourite word in chapter 1 has been 'great': 1:2, 4, 10, 12, 16, 17. In

this 'psalm', that 'great' language has been replaced by language of 'depth' and 'distance'. For instance: 'the belly of the fish' (1:17; 2:1); 'the belly of Sheol' (2:2); 'the deep' (2:3), and so on. This change of language has an effect on the 'psalm': it sets it apart from the rest of the book, and it emphasizes the distress that has come upon Jonah. In turn, this concentration on Jonah's distress emphasizes the determination and power of Yahweh, who uses these means to save him and to get him to obey his will.

2   Sheol (NIV: 'the grave'): a place of desolation, a non-place, a place of distance from God.

Throughout Jonah's 'psalm' there do seem to be allusions to verses of the Psalter. It may help give a 'feel' for this passage to allude to them—you could build them into your group study if you wish. This verse brings to mind Psalms 120:1 and 31:22.

There may be a hint of irony here. Psalm 120:1 starts, in the Hebrew, with 'to Yahweh'. Jonah starts with 'I'. Verses 6 and 9 also have 'I' in pole position. The suggestion is that, in his very despair and contrition, Jonah still remains rather egocentric, a position to which he will revert later.

3   'The deep... the heart of the seas': this double formulation stresses the unfathomable depth and distance to which Jonah is taken. But, of course, that depth and distance is—paradoxically—the very place where he finds God.

We noted last time the catchword 'throw', which occurs at 1:4, 5, 12 and 15. A similar word (NIV: 'hurled') occurs here. Jonah's journey into the depths of the sea and the depths of despair—and his rescue out of that position—is Yahweh's doing throughout. There are allusions here to Psalms 102:10; 69:2; 42:7.

4   Some versions translate 'yet I will

look again...', following the Hebrew text; others translate 'how will I look again...?', following the Greek translation (Septuagint) of the Hebrew Old Testament. The first translation suggests tenacious defiance or longing on Jonah's part; the second suggests despair. Sticking with the Hebrew text seems safer here.

There are allusions to Psalms 31:22 and 5:7.

5   Alludes to Psalms 9:1 and 18:4.

6   Alludes to Psalm 103:4.

7   This is the point of complete despair. Jonah can go no lower without dying. Paradoxically, it is only by being brought so low that Jonah can also be brought to the point of contrition and repentance.

Alludes to Psalms 142:3, 143:4 and 88:2.

8   After the positive response of the foreign sailors in 1:16, Jonah has perhaps learnt something, but learnt it rather late in the day!

Alludes to Psalm 31:6.

9   Allen (page 219): 'Both chapters 1 and 2 end with the theme of sacrifice and vows. The narrator by his inclusion of the psalm immediately after chapter 1 slyly intends his audience to draw a parallel between Jonah's experience and that of the seamen. Both faced a similar crisis... both cried to Yahweh... both were physically saved; both offered worship. Ironically Jonah is at last brought to the point the Gentile seamen have already reached... He who failed to pray, leaving it up to the pagan sailors, eventually catches up with their spirit of supplication and submission... A sincere cry to Yahweh is efficacious whether from a pagan... or from one of his own rebellious prophets.'

There are allusions to Psalms 116:17–18; 3:8.

# 4 Jonah 3:1–10

# Even the cattle repent!

## Aims

• To gain an appreciation of the way the narrator has written this passage—and specifically its links, by way of *similarities* and *contrasts*, with chapter 1—and of why he has done so.

• To reflect on the nature of God's forgiveness, of people's repentance and belief in him, and of the role of God's servants in that process.

• To assess our local church's mission, its strengths and weaknesses, and to consider how this passage addresses those practical issues.

The first parts of this study are more about the text. The last part is more about the setting in which we live and work. The first part is important. But don't spend so much time over it that you don't get to the last part, where the real meat of this study lies!

## Overview

In the introductory leader's notes we saw how there is a *parallelism* between 1:1–16 and 3:1–10. In other words, the passages have been carefully written so as to be compared with each other. There

are various links between these passages:

• They both involve God, Jonah *and non-Israelites* (whereas chapters 2 and 4 centre on just Jonah and God);

• In each case, the non-Israelites are put through a difficult time (the sailors and the storm, the Ninevites and the proclamation of judgment), and in each case their situation is resolved favourably (the sailors worship God, the Ninevites repent);

• In each case Jonah is put through the mill also: in chapter 1, he is thrown into the sea; in chapter 3 the Ninevites repent, leading (in 4:1) to great displeasure on Jonah's part.

This parallelism between chapters 1 and 3 is deliberate on the narrator's part. It is cleverly executed. And it is vital for an understanding of this session's study.

This parallelism is worked out through similarities and contrasts between 1:1–16 and 3:1–10. They can be seen in the very first three verses of chapter 3, where the parallels concentrate on the dealings between Jonah and God.

## Study passage (Jonah 3:1–3)

Jonah 3:1 is exactly the same as 1:1, except that 'son of Amittai' is replaced by the single Hebrew word 'a second time'. The result is that we are meant to note that God's call on Jonah remains the same, despite the events of chapters 1 and 2; also, that call has come again. Jonah is back to square one, but is given another chance!

Jonah 3:2 stresses the persistence of God's call by repeating the very same words as 1:2: 'Arise, go to Nineveh, that great city, and proclaim...'. Yet there is contrast as well: in the next few words, we discover, first, that Jonah is to proclaim 'to' Nineveh and not 'against' it (as in 1:2), and, secondly, that God has a message to Nineveh through Jonah. All of a sudden, God's plans begin to admit of a more benign interpretation. The possibility of communication between God and the Ninevites becomes rather less remote. We find ourselves asking: God has done well through Jonah by the sailors—might he repeat this with the Ninevites? Jonah is back at square one, but this time we know a little more of God's nature and purposes!

Jonah 3:3 starts off in exactly the same terms as 1:1: 'And Jonah arose...' But then we get the big contrast. In 1:3, Jonah got up to run away; here, he gets up...to go to Nineveh! Though Jonah continues to act petulantly later, he is not precisely the same person as he was before the storm and the great fish. Just to rub it in, we are told that he went to Nineveh 'according to the word of the Lord'. Jonah may be back at square one, but he has changed!

Even so, some things (apparently) don't change! Nineveh is still (3:3) a large city. Nineveh remains the archetypal 'big city', a place of wickedness. As we can imagine, Jonah's troubles aren't yet over! He has to proclaim a message to this huge, wicked city: so what will happen?

---

### Study passage (Jonah 3:4–10)

From dealing solely with the relations between God and Jonah in 3:1–3, the narrative now considers the triangle of relationships between *God, Jonah* and *the Ninevites*.

Jonah goes into the city and starts proclaiming. For the first time, in 3:4, we learn the content of his proclamation. Another similarity follows: amazingly—just as the sailors' response was amazing—the Ninevites repent!

There is *irony* here. On the one hand, the Ninevites act a lot more promptly in obedience to God than Jonah ever did. On the other hand, their very repentance results from Jonah's message to them, which is, after all, the fruit of his (admittedly late) obedience! God insists on using the reluctant Jonah, and does great things through even him! The narrator stresses this irony by repeating a key word. First, Jonah is seen as God's agent: Jonah proclaimed (3:4: *qar'a*, 'call, proclaim') God's message... and in response the Ninevites proclaimed (3:5: *qar'a*, 'call, proclaim') a fast! But, also, Jonah is seen as God's reluctant and disobedient agent: in 1:6, the captain told Jonah to 'call' upon his god, and he failed to do so. Jonah only gets around to 'calling' upon God in direst straits, in 2:2. In contrast to Jonah—and yet, paradoxically, in response to Jonah's oracle—the

Ninevites are so keen to respond to God's message that they 'call' twice: first they proclaim ('call') a fast (3:5); then they are commanded to 'call' upon God (3:8). The narrator puts the Ninevites alongside the sailors when it comes to responsiveness to God; Jonah, sadly, gets nowhere close to them—though he is, ironically enough, the human cause of their repentance.

The similarities and contrasts continue. When the message gets to the king, his response is... to arise, get up! The text uses the same word as God uses to command Jonah in 1:2 and 3:2, and the very same word that is used of Jonah when he got up to flee (1:3) and when he got up to obey (3:3). The point is this: the king of Nineveh, non-Jew though he is, immediately gets up and obeys on hearing God's word, whereas Jonah has taken his time about it! Who is the more obedient—Israelite prophet, or heathen king? Yet whom does God use to enable the heathen Ninevites to repent?

## Jonah's oracle

Jonah's message is brief, almost curt. To Jonah and the Ninevites the message was undoubtedly a message of doom. Though the message was understood as one of doom, there *is* an element of mercy within its very wording, since it allows a breathing space of forty days. This is inserted very reticently. Nothing much is made of it. But it is there—a space, a 'tension-laden interval' (Allen, page 222), is conceded.

## The chapter's purpose

For the original hearers or readers, the content of this passage must have been demanding and threatening. We are used to the notion of repentance by non-Israelites. Jewish readers will not have been. They have been exposed to the notion of a reluctant, disobedient Jewish prophet, whom, strangely, God insists on using through his very disobedience. Now they find that a heathen nation repents *en masse* in response to that reluctant prophet's message! Wolff (page 156) comments: 'This scene is an exposition of what it means to arrive at belief in God—an exposition designed to shock its readers.'

The Ninevites come to belief by way of repentance. That repentance happens because of a message of doom. That message is an ultimatum—but one with an in-built space. The time limit acts as a final date, stressing the gravity and certainty of God's judgment. But it also acts as an opportunity for repentance, stressing the possibility of God's mercy.

But how are repentance and forgiveness related? According to the narrator, repentance, though it makes room for God's forgiveness, does not automatically trigger it. God remains a free agent. His forgiveness is just that—his to give and to withhold.

Why face Israel up with an example of non-Israelite repentance, and in such dramatic terms?

41

Perhaps to jolt the original readers into an experience of true repentance and belief for themselves. Maybe it can fulfil the same function for us today also.

## Verse-by-verse

3   The title 'king of Nineveh' is anachronistic: Nineveh was never a city-state in itself, nor was it the capital of Assyria (the state in question) at the time of the historical Jonah-ben-Amittai. The narrator seeks here to convey the impression of a huge city-state, full of wickedness and might. His aim is to make its repentance appear all the more astonishing.

The reported size of Nineveh is unlikely to be historically accurate. It would be 40 or more miles across. Archaeological findings suggest that Nineveh was never more than three to five miles wide. Wolff (page 148) suggests: 'The reader is not supposed to do arithmetic. He is supposed to be lost in astonishment, so that he can take in the events that follow in an appropriate way.'

5   Here is a summary of the contents of verses 6–9. The Ninevites believed God, they proclaimed a fast (see overview notes), and all put on sackcloth. Although the word used is different, as is their consequent behaviour, the Ninevites' response is similar to that of the sailors in 1:16. Significantly, the word for 'believed' is only used positively in the Old Testament of Israel: Psalms 106:12; 119:66; Exodus 14:31; Isaiah 7:9; 2 Chronicles 20:20, for example. It is the word used of Abraham in Genesis 15:6. This attitude of repentance on the part of the non-Israelite Ninevites is meant to astonish and disturb the Jewish reader.

Not only is it astonishing that they repented. What is more, all did so. Martin Luther noted: 'none but saints inhabited the city'.

6   Verses 6–9 fill out and explain the summary statement of verse 5.

NIV and NRSV translates 'the news', which could signify either the news of Jonah's message or the news of the people's response; but the Hebrew ('the word') more probably signifies the content of Jonah's oracle. The king is moved, not primarily by the people's response, but by Jonah's words themselves.

The 'king of Nineveh', who readers would have expected to model arrogant, heathen sinfulness, turns out to be a model of humble repentance.

7   Not only are humans to fast. The animals are to do so also! By this absurd touch, the narrator humorously stresses the extent of the Ninevites' repentance, which contrasts all the more with Jonah's disobedience and subsequent grudging falling into line.

9   Yet these non-Israelites realize that God's forgiveness is not automatic upon repentance. The king's 'who knows?' mirrors the sailor captain's 'perhaps' of 1:6. There is also a clear link with Joel 2:14. This link is made the more likely by the fact that, as we shall see next time, Jonah 4:2 quotes from Joel 2:13. Here, a prophecy applied to Jerusalem, the heart of Israel, is applied to a great heathen city and its inhabitants.

There is another parallel with chapter 1. The captain (1:6) and the king (3:9) both take steps in the hope 'that we do not perish'. Exactly the same words are used in the Hebrew.

10   The language of verse 9 ('turn', 'change mind') is repeated here, stressing that the king's expectation or hope is exactly fulfilled.

Also there is a repetition of words. The word for 'their ways of evil', which the Ninevites turn away from, is the same as 'the destruction' which God turns away from. God takes note here of the Ninevites' turning away from evil, and nothing else.

# 5 Jonah 4:1-11
# Moaning at a merciful God

## Aims

• To explore this chapter's stylistic features and how they fill out and develop our picture of Jonah.

• To explore Jonah's motives and intentions, explicit and hidden.

• To discuss ways in which we (like Jonah) may use doctrine and belief to shield us from the uncertainty and threat of a God who is bigger than us, and to protect us from the needs of others and the difficulties they may present us with.

• To explore how God gently teaches Jonah—and us—a lesson about this.

## Overview

The book of Jonah is written according to a particular structure. For a reminder, see the introductory leader's notes and those to session 4. In summary, chapters 1 and 3 are in parallel, as are chapters 2 and 4. Whereas 1 and 3 have involved God, Jonah and non-Israelites, 2 and 4 concentrate on God and Jonah alone. This spotlighting on God and Jonah shows that chapter 4 is very much about God, Jonah and their relationship. Like chapter 2, chapter 4 is about *Jonah's call by God* and *his response to that call.*

## Contrasts and comparisons

As the narrator has done frequently, he uses comparison and contrast in this chapter. In contrast to chapter 3 (in which Jonah no longer figures after 3:3, and the action then concentrates on the Ninevites), here the spotlight turns to Jonah for the rest of the book, and the Ninevites are out of the picture.

But—and here is the comparison—the Ninevites are not forgotten. The narrator makes links between this chapter and previous chapters. He does this so as to compare Jonah's reactions with those of the Ninevites.

The first of these links comes in 4:1. In chapter 3 we found some repetition of words. One of those words was *ra'ah*. In 3:8 and 10 *ra'ah* was used for the 'ways of evil' which the Ninevites were following. In 3:10 the same word was also used of the 'destruction' which the Lord had threatened and which he turned away from.

In 4:1 we are told that God's merciful actions in 3:10 displeased Jonah—literally '*ra'ah* to Jonah a great *ra'ah*'. The word is repeated, for emphasis. This can be translated as 'This brought a great displeasure over Jonah...'

The point of the repetition is this. The Ninevites' *ra'ah* (their evil) has been overcome by Jonah's message. What's more, God's *ra'ah* (his threatened destruction) has been overcome by the Ninevites' repentance. Now, the narrator asks, what about Jonah's *ra'ah*? By this

43

wordplay, chapter 4 asks the question: can Jonah's *ra'ah* (his anger or displeasure) be also overcome, as their *ra'ah* was? As the study notes put it, Jonah takes it badly that the Ninevites' bad behaviour doesn't lead them to a bad end! We know the Ninevites' reaction to Jonah's message. We know God's reaction to their reaction. But what is Jonah's reaction to God's reaction to the Ninevites' reaction going to be?

So far, then, the passage asks us to compare Jonah with the Ninevites and with God. The Ninevites have changed their minds; God has changed his mind—but will Jonah?

There is more use of this wordplay to come. But first we find another ingredient added to the artistic creation the narrator serves up to us! That new ingredient is the element of surprise.

## A surprise for the reader!

Jonah 4:1 poses the reader a question: Why do God's merciful actions make Jonah angry? So far, the narrator has been very quiet about Jonah's motives. You will remember from chapter 1 how unsure we were as to why Jonah fled. Was it because he was scared? Because he didn't want to give Nineveh the bad news? Because he thought God's doom-laden intentions were excessively harsh? Because it was too much trouble? Because it was a waste of his time? We weren't given any real

information to base a judgment on. But here, very late on in the story, we are given an answer! It was because *he knew all along that God would exercise mercy to the Ninevites!*

This is a surprise. We are forced to re-evaluate the story so far. But it still doesn't resolve all the questions. A new question arises, and it is this: Why was Jonah unhappy with God's forgiving the Ninevites? There are at least two possibilities.

• Jonah, a good Jew, cannot conceive of God forgiving anyone outside the covenant with his chosen people Israel.

• Jonah sees that his mission is a waste of time: if God is going to forgive the Ninevites anyway, why not just do it? Why put Jonah to the trouble of going that distance to give a message of doom which isn't going to come true anyway?

Some interpreters assume that these answers are mutually exclusive. But they aren't. Chapter 4 shows that both issues co-exist in Jonah's mind.

How can we be sure of this? Because Jonah seems to switch between concern for *God* and concern for *himself*. At first, it looks as if he's worried about the character and activity of God. In 4:2 he quotes Psalm 86:15. It looks, at first, as if he is mostly troubled about the idea that God can be this generous to non-Israelites.

But then we wonder. After all, this quotation from Psalm 86 is

44

spoken by an angry man. Isn't Jonah actually using them as an accusation against God? It's as if he is saying: 'You shouldn't be a gracious God, at least not as far as Ninevites are concerned!' And to cap it all, Jonah then moves very swiftly from this statement about God to concern about himself (4:3): 'Please take my life from me.' Isn't the truth that, under the guise of concern about the character and activity of God, Jonah is actually far more worried about himself and his own position?

God discerns this, and asks him, gently: Is it right for you to be angry? Jonah, true to form, doesn't answer, but goes and sulks outside the city, waiting to see what happens next.

So God sets up a *parable in real life* to winkle an answer out of Jonah. And this is where the word-play we looked at above re-occurs.

## More contrasts and comparisons

The word *ra'ah* crops up again. Jonah refuses to answer God and goes and sulks in a booth. There God appoints a bush, 'to save him from his *ra'ah*' (4:6). Most versions translate this as 'discomfort'; but it seems better to translate it as 'displeasure'. God wants to see just what it will take to cheer Jonah up. And, humorously, it takes very little to do so! Once the bush gives him shade, Jonah (literally) 'joys a great joy at the bush'. Having *ra'ah*ed a great *ra'ah* at the generous acts of

God, he joys a great joy at the small matter of a bush. What is really bothering Jonah? He seems most concerned about his own position, and not that of God!

So we get the following. The Ninevites turn from their *ra'ah*. So God turns from his *ra'ah*. This *ra'ah*s to Jonah a great *ra'ah*. He wants to die. So God sees what will get Jonah out of his *ra'ah*. He tries a bush, for shade. It works: Jonah joys a great joy. Then the bush is taken away, and Jonah wants to die again! We see just how sulky Jonah can still be, and the way is paved for God to teach Jonah an object lesson, one which we benefit from as well.

And so, after the 'parable in real life', God repeats the question: 'Is it right for you to be angry...?' But the question has subtly changed. It is no longer—as it was in 4:4—about Jonah's reaction to God's forgiving the Ninevites. It is now about his reaction to the withering of the bush. The point is this: Jonah is as capable of being angry about his own position as he is about the fate of the Ninevites. What, we are led to ask, is the concern closest to Jonah's heart: the plight of the Ninevites, or his own position?

God's repeated question and Jonah's response point up the absurdity of Jonah's position. Jonah is caught in a cleft stick by God's question. If he answers 'No', he would be admitting the folly of his anger over the bush. God's retort might then be, 'Then why be angry about the Ninevites?' If he answers

'Yes', he is asserting that he, Jonah, has the right to be cared for and cosseted by God. And then God might respond, 'If you feel I should look after you, why don't you want me to look after the Ninevites?' A dilemma for Jonah, pointing up the absurdity of his position.

And this is the lesson God drives home and leaves Jonah with. If Jonah is concerned for the bush—albeit for the wrong reason!—shouldn't he be the more concerned for the Ninevites?

## The purpose of the chapter

The developments in this chapter take us by surprise. We find out that, all along, God and Jonah have known why Jonah fled from God. The only people in the dark have been us, the readers. So we are forced to re-evaluate Jonah's actions and motives. We see that, after all, he appears to have been concerned about God's nature and activity in forgiving non-Israelites.

But then we realize that this is a smoke-screen. Wolff (page 176) calls it a 'mock theological battle'. Jonah is actually far more concerned about protecting his view of God, and with protecting himself from inconvenience and surprise. He wants to contain God. The idea that God may be bigger than his understanding of him disconcerts Jonah. Jonah resists that idea. The reader is left with the question: to what extent do we want to whittle God down to our size, to make him manageable, to domesticate him, so

that he demands nothing too difficult, too challenging, too unexpected from us?

## Verse-by-verse

2  One can track Israel's confession of God's compassion through Psalms 86:15; 103:8; 145:8; Exodus 34:6; Nehemiah 9:17, 31; Joel 2:13. In Jonah's mouth, however, these words are accusatory and self-serving.

3  Jonah tries to strike the noble pose. But he fails. His despairing request is reminiscent of Elijah at 1 Kings 19:4 and of Israel at Exodus 14:12. There may be irony here: Elijah is suffering from persecution; Israel is about to be attacked by Pharaoh; and Jonah's trouble? He is suffering from success that he did not want!

6  There is more than a touch of the whimsical in the narrator's picture of God. The great creator and sustainer of the universe has already 'appointed' a fish to teach Jonah a lesson (1:17); now he 'appoints' a bush for the same purpose!
The plant is probably *ricinus communis*, the castor oil plant.

7  The game continues: the bush is attacked by a tiny worm. It only takes a tiny worm to destroy Jonah's happiness!

8  Jonah repeats his complaint of verse 3. But this time the cause seems rather more petty and self-centred. The narrator hints that Jonah is, after all, less concerned about God's activity and its effect on the Ninevites, and more concerned about his own position.

9  This insight is mirrored and strengthened by the repetition of God's question, but this time about the bush.

(NB The 'wordplay' in the study notes is: The Ninevites repented, God relented, Jonah resented!)

# Exodus: From slavery to service

# 1 Introduction

Study notes: Exodus

In this and the next six sessions we're going to take a look at the book of Exodus. There's a lot in the book of Exodus, and we can't hope to cover it all. There's so much that we can't hope to see everything there is to be seen. We will have to be selective.

## Slavery and service

Perhaps the idea of spectacles will be helpful here. With one set of lenses, you might be able to see some things and not others. With another set of lenses, you might see different things, but perhaps not the things you saw with the first ones! Think of bifocals, for example. What you see depends on the lenses you use.

The twin lenses in our spectacles for this unit will be the related ideas of *slavery* and *service*. We are going to see how, in the story of the Exodus, Israel moves from a position of slavery to Pharaoh to a position of service to God. And we are going to explore what that movement from slavery to service meant to Israel, and what it might mean in the modern world, for us and for others. In doing that, we will be thinking about what *salvation* meant (and means) for the Jewish people, and what it means for Christians and for others who live in the modern world.

## What's in a word?

In the course of our study, we will discover that the book of Exodus uses a particular word to describe both slavery and service. It is the verb '*abad*. In Hebrew, it can have a range of meanings, from 'to work', through 'to serve', to 'to worship, obey'. Because this word can bear a whole range of meanings, it is a fruitful way of describing the *continuities* between Israel's slavery to Pharaoh and their service to, and worship of, God, and also the *differences*. We will come across this word later.

These sessions are, therefore, going to be all about *slavery*, *service*, and *salvation*. For our introductory exercise, we're going to start exploring the idea of slavery. The first study will then take that idea further.

### Introductory exercise

• If your group is large enough, split into groups of 3 or 4 people each, to enable discussion. (If you do this, you may want to allow for feedback at the end of the exercise.)

*a)* • Think of some synonyms for slavery. You might like to write them down.

*b)* • Think of some words describing the opposite to slavery. Write them down also.

*c)* • Decide together upon two or three examples of slavery in the modern world. Scan a newspaper or several different newspapers for current examples. It would be good if at least one came from your local or national context and one from further afield. Be as specific as you can.

• Discuss together: how must it feel to be in a position of slavery? Explore together some of what people in this position might feel and how they might react. Relate this to the examples you have chosen.

• How must it feel to be in a position where you hold others in slavery? Explore this too. Relate this to your examples.

• Note how the ideas of slavery and service have *similarities*. In English, for example, another word for slavery, 'servitude', is related to the word 'to serve'. There are other similarities too. But they are also very *different*. Discuss: In what ways are they similar? How are they different? What are the differences between them?

We are now in a position to look at the first study, a story of the children of Israel in slavery…

---

a) subjection (of one person to another).
   intimidation
      oppresion
b) freedom
   democrasy

c) child labour in 3rd. world
   within drug culture (blackmail)
   prostitution esp. of children
   women in some Islamic countries
   status of daughters-in-laws/wives in Pakestan

# Whom will Israel serve?

P.59

## Setting the scene (Exodus 1:1–7)

Verses 1–5 pick up the story of Jacob's sons from Genesis 46 onwards. When Jacob brought his family into Egypt, they numbered seventy people. But, by the beginning of Exodus, that family has become a people. This is no longer a story about God's dealings with a family, but a record of God's dealings with a nation. We're no longer talking family history—all of a sudden we're talking politics.

According to Exodus, the change from family to nation is God's will. Compare Genesis 1:28; 12:1–3 with Exodus 1:7. God has begun to fulfil his promises—but, strangely, that will mean suffering and persecution.

Think of times you have known when God's keeping his word seems to involve pain and setbacks. Share some of this, if you can. Why does God seem sometimes to work this way?

## Will Israel serve Pharaoh? (Exodus 1:8–14)

The setback comes with a new Pharaoh. We aren't told his name. We're just told what he's like. He's an oppressor. Look at his reasoning in verse 10. Where are the flaws in it? What is motivating this line of reasoning?

Discuss a modern example of an oppressor: what motivates them? Why do they do it? Does Pharaoh's reasoning apply to them?

Israel are oppressed by forced labour. Strangely, they thrive. Egypt learns to dread them, and persecution increases. A cycle of blessing and op-pression sets in. The more Israel thrives, the harder the yoke becomes. Where is God in all of this? He doesn't seem very active! Relate this to your modern examples of slavery or oppression. Sometimes God may not seem very active there either. Is the situation then hopeless?

## God's 'strong weakness' (Exodus 1:15–22)

Pharaoh increases the pressure, by planning genocide. The irony is that later it is Egypt's first-born who will die. And, though Pharaoh intends to spare the women, it is they—Moses' mother and Pharaoh's own daughter!—who will thwart his plans. The great Pharaoh tries to get the lowly Hebrew midwives to do his work, but even that backfires.

- The midwives are named, but Pharaoh isn't. Why, perhaps?

- What is the midwives' motivation? How is God at work here?

- Relate this to your modern examples of slavery. How might God act in these circumstances. Through what kinds of people? Be specific.

- Read 1 Corinthians 1:18–28. What hope can this give to people suffering oppression today? Does Christianity merely offer them spiritual comfort in their slavery, or something perhaps more radical?

---

### Or will Israel serve the Lord? (Exodus 2:23–25)

So far Pharaoh seems to have had the upper hand, with God in the background. Yet Moses has survived and been brought up as royalty. But, in frustration, he overreaches himself and becomes an outcast. But things are set to change. Pharaoh's death triggers this change. So far, God has worked in humble ways. Now, he starts acting more openly.

Are there times and places today where God seems able to work only in humble ways? And times and places where he seems able to work more openly? Is this a limitation upon the power of God? How does this fit in with our modern examples of oppression?

Israel cries out. Those cries rise up to God. God hears, remembers, looks, and takes notice  (in Hebrew, God 'knows'). Compare the new Pharaoh and God. Pharaoh doesn't know Joseph or Israel: 1:8. So he oppresses God's people. But God does know his people: 2:25. And, because he is God, he will act.

Relate this to your modern example of slavery. Oppressors do not know their people and do not care. Christians believe, however, that God does. But how is the truth of God's love and care relevant to poor, starving, downtrodden people today? *What is the good news for them?*

So chapter 2 ends on a gentle note of hope. Whom will Israel serve?

---

### A response

- Spend some time quietly pondering what you have discussed.

- In the quiet, have somebody read out Luke 4:16–21. *P.80*

- Use the words Jesus quotes from Isaiah as a basis for intercessory prayer. Pray for the poor, the starving, the oppressed of the world. Pray for the situations you have talked about so far in your discussion.

---

**GROWTH POINTS**

Exodus 3:1–22

# 2 Meeting a holy, concerned God

## Meeting a holy God (Exodus 3:1–6) P.61

• Moses is away from home, exiled, disappointed in his expectations. Why has God chosen to act now?

• God appears to Moses—but in flames which do not burn the bush, and somewhere which Moses is told to treat as holy. What do you understand 'holy' to mean? What does this suggest about the character or nature of God?

• How much awe, or reverence or fear of God is there in our worship of him? In our daily life?

## Meeting a concerned God (Exodus 3:7–9)

But there is more to this passage than God's holiness. We were told last time, in 2:23–25, that God saw, heard, remembered and took note of (knew) his peoples' plight. Three of these words are found here too: God *sees* their misery, *hears* their cry and *knows* their suffering.

• In what way does God know their suffering? Does it affect him in any way? Can we speak of God in such terms?

• Contrast the pictures of God here and of Pharaoh in 5:5f. How are they different?

• Refer to Isaiah 53:3. Christians interpret this text as applying to Jesus, himself God. The suffering servant is (in the Hebrew original) 'a man of *suffering* and *knowing* infirmity'. What light might this shed on the God of Exodus 3:7–9? What was the ultimate consequence for God of being involved in his people's suffering?

• Exodus speaks of God as both holy and moved to compassion by his people's plight. How can God be both holy and vulnerable? How might these aspects of God fit together? Which aspect do you find easier to accept?

## Called to cooperate with God (Exodus 3:10–12)

The apparition in a burning bush serves to reveal God and to conceal him. Because he is holy, he remains ultimately beyond complete knowledge. But, because he is concerned for his people, he reveals something of himself to them and involves himself in their history. In these verses, God announces that he will use Moses to fulfil his purposes. *But why?*

• Suppose for a moment you were God! You have seen the anguish of your people, oppressed by a despot. How would you act to deliver them? How does God act?

• Take one of the examples of servitude you chose last time. If you were God, seeing the anguish of these people, how would you act? How do you think God may in fact be acting in this situation?

• What might be the responsibility of God's servants in such a situation?

• Why should God bother using fallible human beings to carry out his purposes?

God wants Moses to act for him. Moses hasn't expected this! He has already responded, 'Here am I!' But now, faced with God's command, he responds: 'Who am I...?' To encourage him, God assures him: 'I will be with you.' And he offers him a sign.

• When will this sign come to fulfilment, and what must Moses do before it can happen? What kind of sign is it? What response towards God does this sign require of Moses? *must obedience*

• Think about something God has asked you to do. What sort of response was required of you then? Can you say that God was with you in the doing of it? What, if anything, confirmed this to you?

---

### The name of a holy, concerned God (Exodus 3:13–17)

Moses wants further information. We explore his request and God's response.

• How does God respond to Moses' request for information, and why? What might this suggest about the 'working relationship' between them?

• How might this relate to our 'working relationship' with God? Are we permitted to question him? How might he respond?

God's response is very tantalizing! 'I am who I am' could mean 'I will be who I will be', or even 'I am who I will be'! The word often translated as 'the LORD' is related to the Hebrew for 'I am–I will be'.

*yahweh*

• Why did Moses want to know God's name? A simple request for information? Something deeper?

• What does God's name reveal about him? Why should God be willing to make himself known to Moses and Israel? What might be the dangers in this?

• What does God's name conceal from Moses? Why should God conceal aspects of himself from Moses and the people? *P.130*

• John 8:58 records Jesus as telling the authorities: 'before Abraham was, I am'. This is a claim to divinity. God revealed himself preeminently in Jesus. What does Jesus tell us about God, his nature and his concerns?

---

### Working with a holy, concerned God (Exodus 3:18–22)

God encourages Moses: the Israelites will listen. But there will also be difficulties: Pharaoh will resist. But eventually he will let God's people go.

• Will Moses' actions be enough to rescue Israel? What else will be needed?

• Are there times in your ministry or that of the church when both human action and divine action are needed to get something done? Think of examples.

• Would these things have happened without human action? Or without divine involvement?

• What might this suggest to us about the nature of God's involvement in the salvation of the world? How are Christians involved in this? Why does God choose to involve us?

---

### A response   *P.44*

• Read Matthew 28:16–20 together. Because God is a concerned God, he is with us in Jesus as we co-operate with him in serving the world.

• Pray for the needs of the area where you live or work. Pray for the needs of people around you.

• Pray together for activities and ministries your church is involved in as it serves the community.

• Pray together for the ways in which you as individuals co-operate with God in serving others. Ask for his help and his grace.

---

 **GROWTH POINTS**

388 – *Jesus we* *enthrone you*

**Exodus 10:1—11:1**

# 3 Plagues: God's battle with Pharaoh

These are the eighth and ninth of ten plagues visited upon Egypt. Last time we saw how God began to intervene to save his people, promising to act both through Moses and through signs and wonders. Here, God works in both ways (verse 1). But why plagues? We explore why God afflicted Egypt, why Pharaoh's heart was hardened, and whom Israel was to serve.

---

### The plan behind the plagues (Exodus 10:1–2)

Actually, Exodus calls them 'signs', not plagues. Signs are addressed to people, and they are meant to *communicate* something. These signs are addressed to the *Egyptians*, to the *children of Israel*, and to their *children and grandchildren.*

---

### The children of Israel

• God's people still have much to learn of him and his ways. And they are still in bondage in Egypt. The signs contain a *message* for Israel. What is it? Explore this by discussing 6:2–8 together. *p.64*

• What change in attitude are these signs designed to bring about in the children of Israel?

• What understandings of rescue from slavery and freedom from oppression may be present in discussions between Israel and the people of Palestine today? On the side of the Palestinians? On the side of the Israelis? What has given rise to the present position? Might there be room for changes of attitude?

---

### The Egyptians

• What is the message for Egypt in 10:1–2? Explore this through these verses: Exodus 7:5; 7:17; 8:10; 8:22; 9:14; 9:29.

• What changes in attitude should these signs bring about in Pharaoh? In what ways should that change in attitude affect his treatment of others and his exercise of kingship?

• Apply this to one of your modern oppressors. How should their attitude change? How should that change be reflected in their treatment of others?

### Israel's children and grandchildren

• In a sense Christians are 'Israel's children and grandchildren' and heirs to the promises to Israel. What then is the message *to us*? In what ways does the Church need to take this message more to heart?

• God's purposes go even further. Read 9:16, 29. What is the message for 'all the earth' within these signs? What message might they convey to the world today?

### Whom will Israel serve? (Exodus 10:3–20)

The Egyptians 'made the people serve with rigour' (1:13). God has intervened, and his demand is: 'Let my people go, so that they may serve me' (10:3; 4:23; 7:16; 8:20; 9:1; 9:13). Moses' immediate demand is for Israel to celebrate a worship feast (10:9). But the underlying demand is for release from slavery into God's service (10:11). This cry of 'Let my people go that they may serve (worship) me' becomes more insistent with every repetition and every worsening plague.

• How were worship and service linked for Israel? Israel was obliged to worship God while serving Pharaoh. What did God want for Israel?

• How might worship and service be linked for us today? In what ways do we offer worship to God while offering our service to something or somebody else? What does God want for us?

• For the first time (10:7) Pharaoh's officials turn against him; for the first time (10:9, 16–17) he wavers. But even now (10:10–11) he refuses to repent. Presumably God could force his hand. But he doesn't. So, a difficult question arises: Why so many plagues? Why doesn't God deal with Pharaoh more quickly?

• One of the plagues story themes is Pharaoh's hardness of heart. In 4:21, which summarizes the story, it is *God* who is to harden Pharaoh's heart. So also in 7:3. But, from the start of the plagues until chapter 10, we are told either that 'Pharaoh's heart was hardened' or that '*Pharaoh* hardened his heart': 7:14; 8:15, 19, 32; 9:7, 34, 35. But then 10:1, 20, 27 talk again of *God* hardening Pharaoh's heart. Who is responsible?

- Exodus says that Pharaoh's stubbornness is partly God's doing. Why should God choose to harden Pharaoh's heart when that will mean such suffering?

- Yet Pharaoh also bears responsibility. He is not just a pawn in God's hands. How could these two ideas—God hardening Pharaoh's heart, Pharaoh hardening his own heart—fit together?

- Refer back to your modern tyrant. To what extent is God responsible for the continued tyranny of a Saddam Hussein? Could the wickedness of a Hitler be part of the purposes of God? Or was God's heart-hardening activity with Pharaoh a unique event?

- To what extent is your modern example responsible for his own actions? How might *free will* and the *rule of God* over the universe both be true? To what extent does evil have its own way in our world, and to what extent is it under the sovereignty of God?

- The change of language in chapter 10 ('God hardened...') suggests that Pharaoh's attitude becomes so engrained that he can no longer react in any other way. Is it true that oppressive behaviour becomes a vicious circle, reinforcing itself? Apply this to your modern example.

---

### The plague of darkness (Exodus 10:21–29)

Pharaoh nearly caves in now, but he insists on one proviso: the flocks and herds must remain. But Moses won't negotiate. Everything must go! Pharaoh won't agree and dismisses Moses.

- Why is Moses so insistent? Would it not have been prudent to compromise at this point? What is Pharaoh's state of mind at this point? Has he accepted God's sovereignty yet?

- To what extent should modern Christian leaders follow Moses' approach in their dealings with oppressive regimes and situations today? When should we be prepared to negotiate? When should we be willing to compromise? When should we stand by our principles? Apply this to your modern example of oppression.

---

### A response

- Spend some time quietly together, pondering what you have been discussing. P. 592

- Have someone read Psalm 96 out loud.

• Use this psalm as a way into prayer. Give thanks to God for his lordship in Jesus Christ over the universe and over the nations. Pray that rulers and peoples will come to serve him. Pray for places and peoples where there is sadness, evil and oppression. Pray that all the earth may tremble before him and that the nations will ascribe to God the glory due to his name.

## GROWTH POINTS

'Ascribe greatness' 40

48
'Be still + Know
that I am God'

to read / pray
606 'soften my heart'

# 4 Exodus 12:1–36
# Salvation and worship

### New beginnings (Exodus 12:1–2)

God's rescue of Israel was to be the date on which their annual
calendar was to start. The Exodus was a new start, geographically
(they were to leave Egypt), politically (they were to be a separate
nation, no longer under Pharaoh's rule), religiously (they were to
serve and worship God alone). That new start was to affect
everything—even the calendar.

• Israel seemed to make no distinction here between its religious and
its secular life. Does modern society? Do we? Why? Should we?
How much is such a distinction a valid one?

• Our calendar is affected by Christianity—think of Christmas and
Easter. But how far are we really willing to allow the fact that God
has rescued us affect everything we do? Are there areas of our life
still untouched by our faith? What are they? How can we let God
into them?

### Instructions for the Passover (Exodus 12:3–13; 21–23)

These verses report God's instructions to Moses for the original
Passover and the instructions Moses gave Israel. The lamb was to be
slaughtered at an assembly of all Israel (verse 6). Also, it was to be
eaten by households, or more than one if the household was too
small (verse 4).

Israel's rescue was a community affair. They were to be rescued as a
nation: 7:4. They were to listen to God's instructions as a nation:
verse 3. They were to slaughter the lamb as a nation. They were to
eat it as households. God's judgment was a social affair as well: it
was to affect every Egyptian family: verse 12. How much do we see
our salvation as an individual affair? How much should we see it in
those terms? How much should we see it in social terms?

Where does our and society's individualism come from? How far is
it—and an emphasis on personal conversion which goes with it—
essential to the gospel?

In Genesis 22, God showed that Abraham's first-born belonged to
him. In Genesis 22:12 we are told that God spared Isaac since

Abraham had not withheld him, his only son, from God. In this story, Pharaoh will not recognize God. Worse even than that, he has oppressed Israel, God's first-born (4:22–23). The punishment fits the crime: Egypt's first-born shall die.

Apart from the blood on the doorposts and lintels, Israel's first-born would have died too. It represents life given, so that Israel's life may be saved. Why couldn't Israel simply have been spared this as they were spared earlier plagues?

## Passover and holy communion (Exodus 12:14–20; 24–28)

These verses report God's instructions to Moses about the annual celebration of the Feast of Unleavened Bread, and Moses' words to Israel about the annual celebration of the Passover. They are to be a 'lasting ordinance... throughout your generations' and a commemoration of the exodus. The exodus is perhaps *the* event of central significance for Israel. For them, Passover and the Feast of Unleavened Bread commemorate that event.

The New Testament draws parallels between Passover and the last supper. Matthew, Mark and Luke all report that the last supper took place as a Passover meal at the Feast of Unleavened Bread. Paul makes a link between Passover and Jesus' death, for Jesus is the Passover lamb: 1 Corinthians 5:7. The holy communion, based on the last supper, extends the significance of the Passover.

• Passover and the Feast are to be a lasting ordinance for future generations (verses 14 and 17), who have no direct experience of the exodus. Is Israel simply to remember the exodus (verse 14)? Or is the exodus, brought into the present by the celebration of Passover, meant to affect them in some way? How are they to know about the exodus, to be moved by it and to celebrate it? How might it affect them?

• We have not experienced Jesus' death directly: we were not there. In what ways might we be moved by that event and celebrate it in our worship? Are we simply to remember Christ's death, or is it meant to affect us in some way? How?

• Holy communion is different to Passover in many ways. But there are strong links. Obviously it has to do with the death of Jesus, the central event for Christians. How central is holy communion to our life of faith? How central should it be? How do you feel about holy communion? Do you find it different to other forms of worship? If so, why? If not, why not?

• To what extent do we regard *worship* as a family affair? How much do we participate in holy communion as *individuals*, and how much as a *community*?

• An important part of the celebration of Passover was the questioning of children, which was to give rise to an explanation of the significance of the celebration (verse 26). Today in Jewish families Passover still involves the children. What is our attitude to our children in our worship? Is there any room for change? How do we involve our children in *holy communion*? What does your church's practice say to them?

---

### Pharaoh defeated (Exodus 12:29–36)

Pharaoh has finally had enough. He tells the people to go, all of them and with their cattle. And they go, not as refugees, but as victors: verse 36.

Refer back to the situation(s) of oppression you decided upon in earlier weeks. What does God's complete victory over Pharaoh have to say to those who are oppressed? Do we see any evidence of rescue from oppression in their cases? What hope does the gospel offer such people? Merely spiritual encouragement and hope in an ultimate destiny, or something more concrete, something more immediate?

---

### A response

• Spend some time quietly pondering what you have been discussing.

*p.75 SING*

• Have someone read Mary's song, in Luke 1:46–55, out loud. In Jesus, whose death and resurrection we celebrate in the eucharist, the powerful are brought down from their thrones, the lowly lifted up, the hungry filled with good things and the rich sent empty away.

• Pray together repentantly about the role we play, as members of rich and powerful nations, in the suffering of poor and powerless peoples. Pray that the poor and the oppressed will be lifted up and satisfied in Christ Jesus.

• Pray together for the children of the church, that we may learn from them and that they may be enabled to participate fully in the life of the Church.

*end with the grace*

## GROWTH POINTS

38 As we are gathered, Jesus is here

~~... breath of God~~

375 Jesus name above all names

*[handwritten: 4.7.00]*

*[handwritten: STORY RECAP]*

# 5 Sinai: In service of a holy God

*[handwritten: p.79]*

### God's rescue (Exodus 19:1–4)

God addresses Moses on Mount Sinai. He reminds him of what he, God, has done, and of what the people have seen.

God's people have experienced God's rescue as a *community*. What experiences of God's salvation do you, as a group, hold *in common*? Discuss this together, and share any particular experiences or insights.

### God's requirements (Exodus 19:5)

God's gift of salvation *comes first*. It is a free gift, but does not come cheap. God tells Moses what he wants of his people: 'now therefore...'.

Obeying God's voice and keeping his covenant didn't just involve keeping the ten commandments. What else did it entail? In groups of two, brainstorm other Old Testament passages about relationship with the land, treatment of foreigners and fellow-Israelites, relationship with God, avoidance of foreign gods. Then share with the whole group what you have discovered. (Leviticus 19:1; 25; Deuteronomy 6:4–5; 11:13–14; 15:1–2, 7–11; 22:1–4; Amos 2:6–8 may get you started!)

The nearest specifically Christian equivalent is probably Mark 12:28–34. How should these words affect our lives? Why should we try to follow these guidelines? With what motive and to what purpose? *[handwritten: P63]*

### The people's responsibility (Exodus 19:6)

Israel is to be 'a kingdom of priests and a holy nation'. In other words, they are to be set apart for God's special purposes; and they are to act as God's agents and representatives in the world.

• Read Deuteronomy 4:5–6. *[handwritten: P.174]* How should Israel's obedience to God's voice and covenant (verse 5) enable them to be a 'kingdom of priests'?

• 1 Peter 2:9 *[handwritten: P.290]* is based on Exodus 19:6 and Isaiah 43:20–21. What does 1 Peter 2:9 suggest about links between the Old Testament nation of Israel and the Christian Church?

• What does it mean to say that Christians are a 'royal priesthood, a holy nation'? What does 1 Peter 2:9 tell us about our primary calling and function? Who are we declaring God's praises to?

*[handwritten: 790 – you are the King of Glory]*

• What significance does this have for our witness as a community to those around us? See 1 Peter 2:12. How can we become involved in the wider community around us so as to be God's agents and representatives—and yet preserve our Christian identity?

## The people's response (Exodus 19:7–8)

Moses reports back to the people, and they respond to God's words. That is not the end of the story. There are failures and setbacks ahead!

What is *our* response as a *group* and/or as a *church* to God's words to Israel and to us? Where are we failing as a holy nation and a royal priesthood? What specific areas of our lives and ministries need addressing here? What, specifically, can we do about these things?

## Meeting a holy God (Exodus 19:9–25)

Preparations are made for a meeting between God and Moses on the people's behalf. These are frightening enough; the appearance of God is terrifying. God is present with his people, but not at their beck and call. God is terrifying, but he remains with his people, his treasured possession. He is *holy* and at the same time *concerned* for them.

• If God is God, why should he bother to spend time with a tiny Middle Eastern nation? And why with us?

• If God has chosen to spend time with them, why should he scare them out of their wits in the process? What is the point of this?

• Keeping the balance between regard for God's majesty and acceptance of his love for us is difficult for Christians too! Which do you feel happier with—God's holiness or God's love? Why? What could you do to redress the balance?

*individual names?*

## A response

*R615*

• If Israel did as God asked, it would remain God's 'treasured possession'. Using Psalm 135:1–4, spend time together praising God for regarding us as his treasured possession.

*Exodus 80*

• Not only has God rescued Israel—he has also 'borne you on eagles' wings and brought you to myself' (verse 4). Read Deuteronomy 32:10–12. Spend time in prayer together meditating on those words. (Perhaps you might read them out slowly, line by line.) Share anything that particularly struck you as you prayed together.

*— P .203*

*Isaiah 42 1–5 do not be afraid*

## GROWTH POINTS

*423 – living under the shadow of his wing*
*782 – worthy, o worthy*

# 6 Sinai: God's terms of service

*p.80*

## God is first, commandments second (Exodus 20:1–8)

Verse 2 encourages Israel to look backwards and forwards. Backwards, Israel sees that God rescued them. Forwards, they see that God is their master, they his servants. Commandments don't come first, but God.

Looking back: were you ever in 'the house of slavery'? What kind of situation was that? Was God there with you? What did you need to be rescued from? Did God act? How? How much of your rescue was down to you and how much to God? (Share this, if you can).

*Read verse 3 and Matthew 22:34–38.* v.33 Here we have a negative and a positive. 'You shall have no other gods before me.' 'You shall love the Lord your God with all your heart...'

Examine the life of your church. Negatively: which of our habits, traditions, activities, ways of doing things, have we allowed to rival God? How do they come about? How could we put them aside? More positively: in which ways do we as a church express our love for God? What sorts of activities are these? How could we set about developing and extending these expressions of love towards God?

*Read verse 7:* God is concerned for his reputation, his good standing, his name. Part of God's purposes in rescuing Israel is 'that my name might be proclaimed in all the earth' (9:16). We must not 'misuse' God's name (NIV). What is a proper use of his name? On what occasions do we use God's name? Are people drawn to God as a result? How could we be better users of God's name?

## Taking a rest with God (Exodus 20:8–11)

The Sabbath principle sounds strange in the busy modern world. Yet it is important—rest is part of God's own work in creation.

'Sabbath is the voice of gift in a frantic coercive self-securing world' (Brueggemann, *The Land*, 1977, page 63). What does a Christian life full of activity say about our view of God and our relationship with him? Is it better, from a Christian perspective, to *do* things for God or to *spend time* with him?

Examine what you do for God, the church and others. Does it leave time for being with God? What does this say about your attitude to God?

How do we set about finding 'quality time' for God without turning that into another project and another burden?

## Loving others (Exodus 20:12–18)

• Read Matthew 22:34–40. Jesus said loving God and others were the two greatest commandments. The ten commandments are, for the Christian, subject to those principles of love. Jesus embodied those principles. Jesus' teaching in the Sermon on the Mount extends the commandments without limit. In what ways, then, do the ten commandments apply to Christians? As rules, guidelines, principles, or what?

• To what extent are the ten commandments and Jesus' interpretation of them applicable or relevant to modern secular society?

• How are we to set about applying them to the complexities of modern society? Take one of these commandments and discuss a modern ethical issue related to it (abortion, euthanasia, materialism, the free market). How obvious are the answers? How do we use the commandments (and the New Testament) in arriving at a Christian approach?

We cannot look at all the commandments in detail. We take just one.

• Verse 12: how are we to honour parents in a society where people get older, people are more mobile and the extended family less important?

• How do we regard older people in our church? How different is the way we act to that of society around us? In what ways could we better fulfil the essence of this commandment in relation to older people?

## A response    P.5 56

• Have someone read Psalm 37:3–6 out loud. Committing our way to God involves trusting him and obeying him. Pray together that God will help you love him more and love others more deeply.

• Read Psalm 37:1–2, 7. In these studies, we have been thinking much about oppressors and the oppressed. Spend some time quietly together in prayer. If it helps, light a candle or place a picture or icon where everyone can see it. Invite God to speak in the silence.

• Then read Psalm 37:8–9. Pray again in silence. Let God assure you that it is he, not we, who is responsible for the destiny of the world.

## Start pondering

Before your next session, think about what you have gained from studying Exodus. Try to sum this up in two or three thoughts to bring with you to the group the next time you meet.

**GROWTH POINTS**

no. 1 — a new commandment

no. 382 — Jesus teckens aslam

# 7 Covenant and calling

Exodus 24:1–11

At the end of the last session, you were asked to spend some time before this meeting to think about what you have gained from your study of the book of Exodus. Spend some time now sharing your insights and experiences.

## Obedience and service

Read Exodus 24:1–11 together. Israel has been rescued out of slavery in Egypt. They have been brought to Mount Sinai. God has appeared to them, terrifying them. He has given them the ten commandments and has called them into his service. Today's reading is about the sealing of the covenant between God and Israel.

By the sealing of this covenant, Israel agrees to live out a life of obedience and service to God.

We can do that today as well. Here's a covenant renewal ceremony taken from the Methodist Covenant Service. You can use it together as a group, or on your own at home.

*I am no longer my own, but yours.*
*Put me to what you will, rank me with whom you will;*
*put me to doing, put me to suffering;*
*let me be employed for you or laid aside for you,*
*exalted for you or brought low for you;*
*let me be full, let me be empty;*
*let me have all things, let me have nothing;*
*I freely and wholeheartedly yield all things to your pleasure and disposal.*
*And now, glorious and blessed God,*
*Father, Son and Holy Spirit,*
*you are mine and I am yours.*
*So be it.*
*And the covenant now made on earth,*
*let it be ratified in heaven.*
*Amen.*

One note: the Methodist service book says: 'The traditional words "Put me to doing, put me to suffering" do not mean that we ask God to make us suffer, but that we desire, by God's help, actively to do or patiently to accept whatever is God's will for us.'

### Taking time together

After the solemn ceremony between God and Israel, the leaders of the people ascended the mountain, saw God, and ate and drank together with him. In doing so they were already enjoying the fruit of that sealed covenant—a closer relationship with God. Why not take the opportunity at the end of this unit to relax together in God's presence?

 **GROWTH POINTS**

# Introduction

## Why study Exodus?

A central concern of Exodus is to retell the story of God's *rescue* of his people *out of bondage* and into *covenant* with him. Without being too simplistic, there seem to be at least three elements to that summary.

1. God's rescue of his people. Here, the theme is essentially that of salvation or redemption. There are benefits to be had from looking at salvation from a fresh perspective. Over the whole compass of Scripture, salvation is a mighty and broad theme. But sometimes Christians tend to restrict the effect of salvation to the 'soul', or to 'spiritual' areas of life, or to life after death. The Old Testament, which is also Christian Scripture, will have none of that. Redemption has, to be sure, a 'spiritual' aspect in the Old Testament. We will find, for instance, that Pharaoh at times represents the forces of evil in Exodus, so that the Plagues are a depiction of a cosmic battle between good and evil. And, above all, salvation is a matter of the people's relationship with God. But salvation is not only a 'spiritual' idea in the Old Testament. It is also a very here-and-now matter. It often has to do with conquest and possession of land or exile, food or hunger, power or powerlessness. To that extent, the Old Testament refuses to divorce the 'spiritual' and the earthly. So much so that such a distinction is quite foreign to it. How we stand with God affects what happens here and now. How we act and who we are here and now has a bearing on our relationship with God.

We will find that Exodus is one of the sources of the Old Testament's reflection on the saving acts of God. The theme of God's redemption of his people is worked out from this book throughout the pages of the Old Testament, and in all sorts of ways: in personal terms, in corporate terms, in social, political, ethical, national terms, in terms of the cosmic and of the individual. So it is worthwhile to go back to a biblical theme we may think we know pretty well and to look at it afresh, perhaps in a different way. That's not to say that we should limit ourselves to what Exodus says about redemption. We must certainly take Exodus seriously, on its own terms. In other words, we must try not to leap too quickly to a New Testament perspective. But, equally, we stand in a long line of tradition which includes the New as well as the Old Testament, so we must adopt a New Testament perspective also. On the whole, though, the aim of these studies will be to look at the theme of salvation in terms of what Exodus says about it, and to refer to the rest of Scripture as appropriate. You are cautioned therefore against jumping into the pages of the New Testament either too early or too frequently during the course of these studies!

2. Rescue out of bondage. 'Rescue' must mean 'rescue out of something'! Exodus understands bondage in very round terms, reducing neither to the 'spiritual' nor to the merely earthly. It affirms that there is a supernatural element to bondage: the plagues again, for example. But it may be that it is the other aspect—the down-to-earth—which we need to stress a little. Exodus insists that bondage or slavery has a here-and-now effect. It works itself out in real, practical ways, earthly ways, ways which cause ordinary people to hurt. The sons of Israel were not only suffering some sort of 'spiritual' oppression: they were being forced to make a quota of bricks in the heat of the sun!

To recognize this means that we ought to resist the urge to spiritualize the idea of slavery. Yes— serving Pharaoh does involve serving, against their will, the forces of evil; but Exodus insists that slavery has an immediate, earthly, consequence, and not just a future, heavenly one.

3. Rescue is not rescue into nowhere, but rescue into somewhere! That 'somewhere' is relationship or covenant with God. But, of course, the picture is a little more complex than that. God is already in relationship with his people, because of his covenants with Abraham and his children. So rescue out of Egypt may be a starting-afresh with God, but it is not a starting-from-scratch. So we must avoid suggesting that this is the first time that God and Israel have been involved with each other. That would be to ignore the book of Genesis. Of course, this is the first time God will have been involved with Israel as a nation: see the first study. So, in that sense, the relationship is a new one. And, what's more, this will be the first time God has revealed himself as 'I am' and the giver of the Law. To that extent the relationship will be very different this time round.

Nor does the book of Exodus suggest that leaving Egypt and entering into God's service is the end of Israel's problems. It is only the beginning! There follows, very immediately, the wilderness experience. Even after the conquest of the land, disobedience and exile will follow.

So we must be careful not to depict slavery and service in stark, black and white terms. Even slavery in Egypt has its positive side: God is committed to the children of Israel. And part of the drama of Exodus is the telling of how the possibilities inherent in that fact become reality. On the other hand, even service of a holy God has its hazards: Israel can never afford to rest on its laurels.

## Other things to bear in mind

There are other issues we need to be aware of in handling this book. First, we need to recognize that there is great diversity in it. But also unity. As far as diversity goes, you will find, for example, story-telling; poetry (chapter 15); law-giving (chapter 20 onwards); detailed instructions for tabernacle-making (chapter 25 onwards). What's more, the scope of the book is huge. Yet within that there is unity. For example, God meets Moses at 'the mountain of God' in chapter 3; and, as prophesied, he returns to the same mountain with the people in chapter 19. This is not accidental: it makes for unity within the book and demonstrates the continuity involved in God's rescue of his people.

One particular aspect of this deserves thought. The first 19 chapters are devoted mainly to story-telling; much of the rest of the book is the giving of Law. How are these two things linked? Perhaps 20:2 is crucial: before the revelation of the Law at Sinai, we read: 'I am the Lord your God, who brought you out of the land of Egypt, out of the house of bondage'. So perhaps we need to interpret the Law aspect in the light of the story. The God who reveals the Law is the God who has rescued his people from bondage into covenant with him. This means that the Law is not an end in itself, but the way in which the covenant with God is regulated and worked out.

Finally, there is the issue of 'particularity'. One of the recent trends in interpreting Exodus has been to think about how it may speak to those suffering ethnic and political oppression in the world today. Liberation theology has particularly taken these ideas up. It would be foolish to deny the considerable power of the insights which result: as we have seen, Exodus will not allow us to 'spiritualize' what it says about slavery and service. So any attempt to interpret Exodus as if it had only to do with our relationship with God or with our final destiny would be to misinterpret it. We need to ask, with people who suffer oppression: What does Exodus have to say to the oppressed today? On the other hand, we must note that the story is about God's rescue of Israel, his chosen people and treasured possession. Israel is not just any nation, but the nation through whom God has decided to work out his purposes. Of course, once we have narrowed the focus like this, we must widen it again. God's purpose is not just to rescue Israel, but to bless all people. Genesis 1:28 and 12:3, which the very first lines of Exodus bring to mind, make this very clear. God's choice of Israel is a particular one, but for a more universal purpose.

This is a complex issue, and one that needs thought. For the moment all we need to do is to note the twin dangers:

• that of interpreting Exodus so narrowly that we deny it has anything relevant or practical to say to peoples crying out under oppressive régimes today;

• that of interpreting Exodus so widely that we lose sight of the claim of the Old Testament that God chose Israel specifically to be the vehicle for his universal purposes.

There is a tension here, and we will have to tread wisely. It becomes an issue in the very first study!

## A note

All of the questions in the study notes are of roughly the same weight, and so there are no 'key' questions. On the other hand, there is plenty of material provided, probably too much to be covered at one session. So you may wish to be selective in the questions you address. Each session does contain the opportunity for a response at the end, and you will want to make sure that you do get to this part of the session.

Exodus 1:1–22; 2:23–25

# 1 Whom will Israel serve?

## Aims

• To reflect on the nature of slavery and to draw parallels between Israel's slavery and experiences of slavery today.

• To consider how human and divine action may together provide hope in situations of slavery, and to relate this to the modern world.

• To reflect on how God often uses weak people to shame the powerful and to carry out his will.

## Materials required

Newspapers (for the activity in the introductory study notes).

## Overview

All that you need to know by way of overview for this session is contained in the introductory leader's notes.

## Verse-by-verse

1   Exodus is not a stand-alone book: it has links with Genesis, and is fully part of the Pentateuch, the first five books of the Bible. At the end of Genesis, the Israelites are called, literally in Hebrew, the 'sons of Israel', and they are exactly that—the sons of Jacob, who was named Israel (Genesis 49:2).
These 'sons of Israel' are named in Exodus 1:1–6, and this provides

continuity with Genesis. But by verse 7 it is apparent that the phrase 'sons of Israel' (the same phrase—NIV blurs this link!) must mean something else, for the 'sons of Israel' are now a people. The family has grown into a people; and, while there is continuity with the history of that family in Genesis, there are also differences, because the way a people is perceived by others is different to the way a family is perceived. And many of Israel's troubles in Egypt stem out of this distinction.

**7** This verse is not merely a statement of fact, though it is certainly that. (1) it picks up the words of God's promises to Adam and Eve in Genesis 1:28. The words for 'were fruitful', 'multiplied' and 'the land was filled' all occur here and in Genesis 1:28. (2) this verse is also meant to remind us of God's promises in Genesis 12. So: this verse represents a partial fulfilment of God's promises. But, ironically, this is also the source of Israel's new problems: its very fruitfulness and nationhood make it appear a threat to Pharaoh.

The Hebrew is very graphic: 'But the sons of Israel were fruitful and swarmed.'

**8** The new king of Egypt is not named, and remains a cipher. He is used by the writer as a representative of evil, oppressive rule. Note the contrast with the Hebrew midwives in verse 15 who, despite their apparent insignificance, are named. Naming is very important, and the lack of a name for Pharaoh is unlikely to be accidental. Later on he will come to typify the forces of chaos in the fight against God.

There is a link between 1:8 and 2:25. The king did not 'know about' Joseph. The Hebrew uses the common word for 'to know' here. Pharaoh's 'not knowing' leads him into all sorts of oppressive behaviour. This is a flexible word. In 2:25, the word NIV translates as 'was concerned about' is the same word in

Hebrew. It is not that God knows something he didn't know before. It is more that he took notice, that he perceived their plight and decided to do something about it. The point is this: for Pharaoh, 'not knowing' leads to oppressive behaviour; for God, 'knowing' leads to saving action. The theme of Pharaoh and the Egyptians 'not knowing' recurs later: 5:2; 6:7; 7:5. Not only does Pharaoh not know Joseph; also, he does not know the Lord, and part of the point of the plagues and of the exodus, as the book of Exodus sees it, is to teach him this lesson.

**9** There is irony here: Pharaoh is the first person to recognize Israel as a people. That nationhood is part of the fulfilment of God's promise to his people. Yet the very act of recognising their nationhood leads Pharaoh to oppress them and thereby to dehumanize and belittle them.

**10** Pharaoh's argument is patently spurious: first, it adds hypothesis to hypothesis. Second, it is illogical: Why should Israel wish to leave the land if they were not oppressed? Pharaoh's very actions and policies bring about the events he professes to want to avoid.

**13** This verse introduces an important theme for our studies. Again, NIV partially obscures the careful writing. The theme or wordplay is that of *'abad*, to serve or to worship. This issue has been mentioned in the introductory study notes. This is a very flexible word. It can denote slavery or service. In Exodus it is used both of slavery to Pharaoh and of service of God, worship of him and obedience to him. In this verse, word for word, the Hebrew reads: 'So they made the people serve with rigour, and made their lives bitter with back-breaking service in mortar and brick and with every kind of service in the field; with every kind of service they made them serve with rigour.' The repetition is deliberate. It raises the question: *Whom will Israel serve?* And, if it is Pharaoh they will serve, *what kind* of service will it be?* The theme of *'abad* provides one of the leading motifs in Exodus.

15 The structure of the passage becomes important here:

• Pharaoh speaks to his people: verse 9

• They respond by oppressing the children of Israel: verse 11f

• Pharaoh speaks to the Hebrew midwives: verses 15–16

• They respond by disobeying him: verse 17f

In this way, the effectiveness of Pharaoh's commands is hinted at. In the short term, the Egyptians' actions seem most effective. But in the long term they carry the seeds of their own downfall: in due course, Egypt's first-born sons are themselves killed. In the short term, the midwives' disobedience seems futile and appears to make matters worse: verse 22. But in the long term their inaction leaves room for Moses to live.

What of the midwives' deception? Is it to be criticized? Would it not have been more immoral to kill the sons? What of Acts 4:19f, where Peter seems willing to disobey instructions of those in authority if they are contrary to the revealed will of God?

17 God is expressly mentioned only here and in verse 20. Until we get to 2:23 God is not at the centre of the storyline. He is there, acting, but unobtrusively, behind the events of the story.

18 Irony again. Pharaoh perceives the midwives' inaction as direct, active disobedience. In fact, they have simply done nothing. Their inaction, despite their lowliness in the face of Pharaoh, is more powerful than all the activity of Pharaoh's minions.

22 More irony. The women, those whom Pharaoh ignores because they seem insignificant, are the very ones who save and nurture Moses and thus enable Israel's salvation to occur.

23 This passage provides a bridge between the story so far and chapter 3. So far the scenario has been bleak, and God has been at work only behind the scenes, and very slowly at that! But, with a change of king, a change in the nature of God's activity is signalled. These verses suggest that the bleak picture of chapters 1 and 2 are not the whole story; and they also herald the event of the burning bush. They suggest that the possible answers to the question, 'Whom will Israel serve?' may not be the answers which have come to mind so far.

# 2 Meeting a holy, concerned God

on God's nature and his activity in history. These two themes are closely related. Who God is, he will reveal himself in history to be. This story links these themes indissolubly together.

## Aims

• To ponder the themes of holiness and involvement and to consider their coexistence within God.

• To think about ministry as a cooperative venture between God and us, and to consider the implications of such ministry.

• To relate both of these issues to the incarnation and what that tells us about God's nature and participation in history.

## Overview

In our passage, God appears to Moses. But this is more than just an appearance. In Genesis, God had already appeared to the patriarchs and revealed his promises to them. But this meeting with Moses goes further: for God tells Moses to go and give a message. Arguably, then, this is the first commissioning of a prophet to be related in the Old Testament. So it has as much in common with the call of prophets such as Isaiah and Jeremiah as it does with God's appearances to the patriarchs.

This story—of a divine *encounter*, the divine *name* and a *sign*— amounts to a theological reflection

## God's nature

While God is holy (3:5), he is also willing to share in the sufferings of those he loves (3:7). Here is a paradox we need to explore. We find the same paradox—between the holy, almighty God and the involved, vulnerable, suffering God—within the pages of the New Testament. Because God is *almighty*, he can ultimately never fully be known by human beings. But, because he is also *involved* in the lives of his people, he chooses to reveal himself to them. This paradox is explored by various means in this story:

• The *divine name* both conceals and reveals: it tells something of who God is, but also insists that God will not be fully known until his purposes are complete. There is room for revelation and for mystery, and that calls forth faith from God's people.

• The *burning bush* reveals God to Moses but also conceals him. The figure in the bush is at the same time very much present and entirely mysterious.

• The *sign* (3:12) reveals and conceals. It is a promise for Moses to grasp; but, because it will only come about after Moses has obeyed

God, it cannot yet be fully grasped. It calls forth *trust* from Moses.

## God's action in history

Our passage asserts that God, because he is almighty, can perform the miraculous. And he will do so again, in the infliction of the plagues. Yet he doesn't choose to act entirely by this means. He is not only almighty. He is also involved in his people's lives. Because of this he chooses to make himself vulnerable to his people. God is willing to act through Moses and *to be constricted by human limitations*. This is the same paradox, seen in a different way. Because God chooses to act partly through Moses, he shows himself willing to be vulnerable to the effects of human sinfulness. Astonishingly, despite God's holiness, Moses argues the toss with God, and God lets him do so. More than that, God only reveals himself by his name because Moses argues the toss with him. Thus this passage is saying something important about the way God calls his servants, works with them and is willing to be bound, to an extent, by their fallibility.

## Verse-by-verse

1 The whole chapter amounts to the beginning of the fulfilment of 2:23–25. In contrast to the behind-the-scenes God of chapters 2 and 3, we find here a God who acts more directly.

'Was tending the flock': past continuous tense: Moses was going about his normal activity.

'Horeb': the mountain of God:
scholars are unclear as to why the same mountain is referred to as Horeb and Sinai. If, as some believe, Exodus is a stitching-together of different source materials, it may be that different names were used in different sources. 'Horeb' is related semantically to the Hebrew for 'waste', 'desolation'. The location of the mountain is uncertain. Many place it at Jebel Musa in the south of the Sinai peninsula.

2 In Hebrew, as in Greek, the same word is used for 'angel' and for 'messenger'. In Old Testament accounts of the appearances of God (theophanies) there is often ambiguity as to whether the apparition is of God's messenger or of God himself. Verse 2 refers to an 'angel' or 'messenger'; verse 4 onwards refers to 'God'; in verse 6, Moses is afraid to look at God. For another example of ambiguity, see Genesis 18.

Burning bushes are not unusual in the desert—but it is usual for the flames to consume them!

Why an appearance in a 'flame of fire'? Fire is at once tangible and intangible. It has a real effect: it consumes, gives off heat. But it cannot be grasped or easily contained. In the flame of fire, God was at the same time truly *present*, and yet not fully *contained* within it. His presence did not mean that Moses could grasp hold of him or manipulate him. God was not bound in any way by his self-disclosure, nor fully contained within it.

5 The ground was holy because it was the place of God's appearance to Moses. Taking off sandals is an Eastern sign of reverence.

6 'The God of Abraham...': this is not God's first dealings with the children of Israel. In verses 7 and 10 he calls them 'my people'. They are already related to him by covenant and by God's promises. By using this formula, that relationship is called to mind, as 2:24

has already indicated.

7 These, almost the first words of direct speech from God in Exodus, set the framework for God's activity and nature for the rest of the book.

His words reprise three of the verbs used of God in 2:24, 25: 'see', 'hear' and 'know'. But here we get more detail. Seeing: this is emphatic: 'Indeed I have seen the misery of my people...'. Hearing: 'I have heard them cry out...'. But, more than this, God *knows their sufferings*. This is more than a mere acknowledgment of their plight. Fretheim (page 60) suggests: 'God is here depicted as one who is intimately involved in the suffering of the people. God has so entered into their sufferings as to have deeply felt what they are having to endure.' But there is one difference with God: while he suffers with his people, he is not powerless as they are in the face of it.

8 God's aim is not to make suffering more bearable, but to rescue Israel from it. And already here we find mention of the Promised Land. This rescue involves a destination.

10 Suddenly it becomes apparent that God intends to use Moses to fulfil these plans! Moses is to be given responsibility. He will not, of course, be without God's help. The signs of 4:30f and 7:8f make that clear. Yet Moses is to be God's agent. Why? Surely God could rescue Israel without his help! There are some deep things about *service* and *ministry* to be pondered here. One line of thought is the issue of free will. God does not choose to impose solutions on his people. They must to some extent remain involved and responsible for what happens. This in turn involves a reduction in God's freedom. In using human beings for his purposes, God in some way and to some extent chooses to set limits on the sovereignty of his activity. This divine willingness to be tied to human frailty

foreshadows—even here in Exodus—the Incarnation.

11 More than this: to send Moses opens God up to the possibility of questioning and prevarication from Moses. On one level, Moses' question is a humble one. On another level, it is less humble, for it casts doubt on God's choice of him.

12 God's response is at once a corrective and an encouragement: 'I will be with you.'

The return to the mountain seems to operate as the 'sign' of the fulfilment of God's promises. This is odd: signs generally anticipate the fulfilment of the promises to which they refer. Here, though, the sign is part of the fulfilment of those promises. Hardly much encouragement for Moses! It may be that, just as the burning bush involves a revelation (of God's presence) and a concealment (of the fulness of God), so this 'sign' involves a revelation and a concealment. God reveals a sign, an assurance that he will accomplish his purposes. Yet within that revelation lies also a concealment, for that sign cannot be fully laid hold of until it happens. That is just as well, for the bringing-about of the sign involves action by Moses, and he is reluctant to act! So the sign both provides Moses with encouragement (that God will fulfil his plans), and calls forth faith from him (for Moses cannot yet grasp the sign). See Isaiah 7:14 for another sign of this sort.

13 We arrive at one of the conundrums of the Hebrew Bible! Moses wants to know God's name, in case the people ask. It is unlikely that this is a bare request for a name, as if the people had forgotten it! There is more to a name than that. In the Old Testament, names are often an indication of a person's character or of events which have shaped a person's life. And that's the nature of Moses' request here: he is

asking to know more about God himself. It is a request to know the significance of God's name.

14 But what does God's response mean? The problem is this. The Hebrew verb used can either mean 'I am' (present) or 'I will be' (future). So there are four options: 'I am who I am', 'I will be who I will be', or permutations of the two. Some see this name as a rebuff: 'mind your own business; who I am is nothing to do with you; just do as I say!' Not convincing. 'I will be who I will be' or 'I am who I will be' are, on current scholarly thinking, the most likely possibilities. If so, we may be dealing with God's revelation of himself in history. It is not so much that God tells Moses who he is in a flash of revelation. It is more that God will reveal who he is progressively over the course of his dealings with Israel. So the story, as it unfolds, will tell us who God is. A quotation from *The Lord of the Rings* by J.R.R. Tolkien may help. Treebeard the Ent replies to Pippin's request for his name like this: 'For one thing it would take you a very long while [to listen to my name]: my name is growing all the time, and I've lived a very long, long time; so my name is like a story.' God is disclosing to Moses something of who he is. But he also holds much back, because *who God is will only truly be seen as the story unfolds*. God is what his activity in history reveals him to be.

On this basis, the same paradox of revelation and concealment as we have seen already in this passage may be operating here. Fretheim (page 65) comments: 'Giving the name entails a certain kind of relationship: it opens up the possibility of, indeed admits a desire for, a certain intimacy in relationship... Naming makes true encounter possible. Naming entails availability... Yet... there remains an otherness, even a mystery, about the one who is named.' Very suggestively, he adds: 'Naming also

entails vulnerability. In becoming so available to the world, God is to some degree at the disposal of those who can name the name.' If so, then there is both an openness and a reticence in the giving of this name. God discloses something of himself, becoming vulnerable and making relationship and closeness possible between him and his people. Yet he also holds something of himself back, refusing to make himself utterly at the disposal of humanity, utterly vulnerable to them. For then how would he remain God?

Strangely, this verb-name, 'I am' or 'I will be', is used as a noun: Moses is to tell Pharaoh that '"I am–I will be" has sent me to you'.

There are two added twists to this use of God's name. First, we have met God's name already! In verse 12, God said 'I will be with you.' The 'I will be' is God's name. So verse 12, looked at from the vantage-point of verse 14, becomes a wordplay. Secondly, the word our versions translate as 'the LORD' in verse 15 is derived from the Hebrew for 'I am–I will be'. 'Yahweh' (Jerusalem Bible version of 'the LORD') is an attempt to reproduce the consonants of the divine name (YHWH) in English. The name (YHWH) which the Old Testament often uses for God contains within it the very name which God reveals at Horeb.

The conversation continues into chapter 4, with Moses raising objections and God accommodating himself to Moses, though not without a gust of anger (4:14)! Amongst much else, chapter 4 shows how far God is willing to go to accommodate himself to Moses' frailty and uncertainty.

# 3 Exodus 10:1—11:1
# Plagues: God's battle with Pharaoh

## Aims

• To consider the reasons given in Exodus for the plagues, and to apply those ideas to a modern setting of oppression and to church life.

• To reflect on how worship and service are linked, and to allow those insights to deepen our service and worship of God.

• To ponder issues of human responsibility before a sovereign God and to examine how those issues might relate to each other.

• To examine Moses' example before Pharaoh and to consider the extent to which it should inform Christian approaches to oppression today.

With the plague account we come to a fascinating and problematic part of Exodus. These notes are to help you work through some of the thorny issues it raises.

Many scholars adopt a theory that 7:8—11:10 started life as a number of different stories about the same events, written at different times, for different purposes and from different theological slants. So we should, they argue, expect to find loose ends and haphazardness in the stitching together of the

story as we have it. That is fine as far as it goes; but it doesn't fully account for the state of the text as we have it today. A more recent approach is to concentrate upon the text as we have it, and to ask why it was put together as we find it. We will be concentrating on that question here.

The first issue is the *structure* of the plague narrative, 7:8—11:10. Is there some pattern to the way it is written? Here are some possibilities. The plagues may be in ascending order of gravity, starting with annoyances, moving to disease and damage, and finally to darkness (the darkness before creation?) and death. Or there may be five groups of two plagues—Nile, insects, diseases, damage, darkness/death. Or three groups of three. Certainly it is worth noting that, in plagues 3, 6 and 9, there are no negotiations with Pharaoh before they take place.

The second issue is this: what is the significance of the *nature* of the plagues? Are they just handy ways of bringing Pharaoh to heel? Or is there a message within the plagues themselves? After all, the text calls them 'signs', not plagues: 7:3. And signs are usually there to communicate something. Fretheim suggests that these signs are not just arbitrary events, but convey their own message within them. He suggests (page 106) that there is a connection between the moral order and the natural order. A breach of God's moral laws involves a threat to the order of creation. So

Pharaoh's oppression gives rise to natural consequences which threaten the stability of nature. To put it another way: God's purposes in creation are to bless all people, not just Israel. The ultimate purpose of his rescue of Israel is not simply to bring Israel out of slavery, but to bless all people through them. There is a close connection between God's purposes in creation and his purposes in salvation. So Pharaoh's refusal to obey God isn't just an attempt to thwart God's immediate plans for Israel. It's not even just an attempt to undo God's salvation plans. *It amounts to an attempt to undo God's purposes in creation.* For that reason, the plagues are an expression of the consequences of his actions.

This suggestion is worth pondering, though it would be going too far to see the plague narrative as a sort of ancient morality play. Pharaoh may in a sense represent the forces of chaos; but he is also a historical person and a character in the story in his own right. He is no cardboard-cut-out figure. The writer depicts his character in some detail.

The third issue: how are we to understand the matter of the hardening of Pharaoh's heart? What is the writer trying to say? Firm answers are hard to come by here. Don't be surprised or concerned if your group doesn't come to any final solutions. Here are some pointers. Sometimes the text talks of God hardening Pharaoh's heart.

See 4:21; 7:3; 10:1, 20, 27. So we might want to ask: does this mean that Pharaoh has no say in the matter? Is he just clay in the hands of God the potter, to be shaped as God wishes? Before we come to this conclusion, we must note that, many times, the text says that Pharaoh's heart became hard, or that he hardened his (own) heart: 7:14; 8:15, 19, 32; 9:7, 34, 35. Does this mean, then, that Pharaoh is entirely responsible for his reaction to Moses and to God?

It looks as if the writer wants us to understand that Pharaoh's obstinacy is both God's plan and Pharaoh's responsibility. And then we are bound to ask how these things relate to each other. At this point we are close to some very substantial questions indeed, though admittedly the text does not address them explicitly or expand upon them. *How does God's rule of the whole of creation relate to the fact of human responsibility and free will?* If Pharaoh is acting in an evil way, where does that evil come from and who is responsible for it—God, or Pharaoh?

Don't expect the group—or anyone else!—to find absolute solutions to these matters. It is enough to begin to discuss them. One further thought may assist. These texts seem to fall into three categories:

• 4:21 and 7:3, where the narrator summarizes things by saying that God hardened Pharaoh's heart;

• the first seven plagues, where the text repeatedly tells us that

Pharaoh's heart became hard, or that Pharaoh hardened his heart;

• chapter 10 onwards, where (apart from one example in 9:12) 'God hardened...' begins again.

Possibly, the writer wants us to see that there comes a point where wrongdoing and disobedience become an engrained, hardened course of action and in that sense irrevocable. At that point the die is cast, and the consequences are fixed. We explore this idea in this study. There is at least one reservation. If this is the case, why is Pharaoh given the chance to change his behaviour in 10:3, 4? It is a matter of judgment whether, by this stage, the prospect of Pharaoh's change of heart is a real one at all.

## Verse-by-verse

2 'How I dealt harshly' (NIV), 'how I have made sport' (RSV), 'how I have made fools' (NRSV): another possibility is 'how I have dealt severely with'.

3 'Humble yourself' (NIV): this is another form of the verb used in 1:11, meaning there 'to oppress'. Are Pharaoh's oppression of his subjects and his failure to humble himself before God linked, not only verbally, but in other ways too?
'Serve/worship': see the study notes. The Hebrew verb 'abad can be translated 'to serve, worship, work, till the soil'. Here the first two meanings are the relevant ones.

7 Note the repetition of 'how long...' in verses 4 and 7, for effect. The plagues have got so bad that Pharaoh's officials, as well as God, are asking how long before Pharaoh gives in! They also repeat the 'Let the people go' of verse 4.

10 Pharaoh's words are probably sarcastic here: 'The Lord indeed will be with you if ever I...' (NRSV).

16 Pharaoh's recognition of his sin may be something—and indeed the response of the lifting of the plague is sudden and startling. Such would be the ultimate outcome if Pharaoh obeyed God. But it quickly becomes apparent that this confession falls well short of recognition of God's rule over his actions.

19 The sweeping of the locusts into the Red Sea may well be a sort of foreshadowing of the fate of the Egyptians in chapter 14.

22 For emphasis, the Hebrew reads 'darkness–thick darkness', a sort of compound word.

26 Here, the primary meaning of 'abad has to be 'worship', because of the context.
Moses' reasoning does seem a little hollow. But this is parleying. Both parties realize that the complete freedom of the Israelites is now the issue at stake. That freedom includes the right to offer worship to God as freely and as completely as they can. Pharaoh rightly sees this desire to offer worship to God as a threat. He knows that the worship of God means for the people of Israel complete obedience to God and a complete dismantling of Pharaoh's own power over them.

29 Literally, 11:4 and 8 make it clear that Moses did see Pharaoh again. But that is probably not the point of this verse. Pharaoh is threatening Moses with death if he ever sees him again. Moses implies in his answer that the boot is on the other foot. Moses is in effect accepting the finality of this meeting and the finality of Pharaoh's decision to thwart God. The outcome, however, will not be at all as Pharaoh would have desired it.

# 4 Salvation and worship

**Exodus 12:1–36**

## Aims

• To consider the modern division between the sacred and the secular and its consequences for society and the gospel.

• To reflect on individualism in society and worship.

• To discuss the place and significance of holy communion.

• To consider the role of children in worship.

• To ponder further what the gospel offers to the oppressed.

Interpretation of the Passover account has been dominated by investigation into the history of the sources thought to have contributed to the final text. Much of this investigation has been speculative. As Childs (page 195) notes: 'The emphasis on the prior history of the biblical text… has often resulted in unwillingness and even inability to read the text in its present form.' It is that final text which we concentrate upon here.

We are able to study only part of the Passover account this session. What is the broader outline of the story? Childs (page 196) sees the account as extending from 12:1 to 13:16. His outline of our part of the story is as follows:

*12:1–20 Speech of instruction to Moses and Aaron, to be conveyed to the people, about preparation for the Passover (12:1–13) and the feast of unleavened bread (12:14–20)*

*12:21–27a Moses' speech to the people, with instructions about the preparation of the Passover and future celebrations of that feast*

*12:27b–28 Response of the people*

*12:29–36 Narrative of the exodus, told from the perspective of the Egyptians.*

Several thoughts follow from this. First, there is a structure visible within our short piece of text. In the instructions to Moses (1–20) there is a slide from the immediate preparations for the Passover (verses 1–13) to instructions for the liturgical celebration of the feast of unleavened bread in years to come (14–20). The same slide takes place in Moses' speech to the people: immediate preparations (21–23) and instructions for later liturgical celebration (24–28). We could represent this in chart form also:

*12:1–20 Instructions to Moses*
*1–13 immediate preparations for Passover*
*14–20 instructions for future celebrations*

*12:21–28 Moses' instructions to the people*
*21–23 immediate preparations for Passover*
*24–28 instructions for future celebrations*

This slide between an immediate, historical focus and a wider, liturgical focus is an important one. It reflects an interplay in the text between salvation as *past event* and salvation as *present reality*. Both of these ideas are found in the text. The focus on the historical events of the exodus stresses salvation as past event. This focus stresses that, from the reader's point of view, Israel's salvation is rooted in objective, independent, historical *events of the past*. On the other hand, the focus on the instructions for the feast in future years stresses salvation as present reality. In rehearsing the events of the exodus in the feast of unleavened bread, Israel—that is, the believer—not only remembers its rescue out of Egypt, but makes that rescue a *present reality* in its life.

This is a difficult but important idea to get hold of. The text is all about the historical events of the Passover and exodus *and* all about how those events are to be remembered and made real and effective in the life of the people of God. Fretheim (page 138) says that the text amounts to an interweaving of liturgy and story. Story and liturgy, salvation remembered and salvation re-enacted, are indissolubly linked in this passage.

The New Testament has an ambivalent attitude to the Passover. On the one hand, it is keen to make links between Jesus' death and the Passover. For example, the synoptic Gospels speak of Jesus eating a Passover meal before his death. It is clear that those Gospels regard the last supper as a Passover meal. On the other hand, the New Testament also understands Jesus' death as fulfilling and hence setting aside the Old Testament observance, of which Passover is part.

So holy communion has many links with the Passover, though it is fair to say that the accounts of the Lord's supper draw also on other Old Testament traditions (such as the one about the Messianic banquet at the end of the age: see Mark 14:25). In this study we draw upon the links between Passover and the eucharist and use that as a way into discussion about *what we are doing in worship*. One interesting line of thinking is that worship actualizes (brings into the present) significant historical events and their significance for us. For example, the holy communion doesn't just remind us of Christ's death and resurrection and the significance of those events for us—though it does do that. It also brings those events and their significance into the present and *makes them effective for us*. The eucharist isn't just a memorial meal, but an effective channel of God's grace. These insights may help give some depth to our understanding of Exodus 12 and of holy communion.

## Verse-by-verse

1   So significant is this event to be, as a new start for the people, that the annual calendar is to commence from it.

2   The prescription of the Passover and the feast are precisely set out, and involve 'all the community of Israel' (verse 4). A brief summary of the celebration of the Passover after the exodus is as follows: Israel kept the feast at Gilgal on entering the Promised Land (Joshua 5:10f.). Passover was re-instituted in the time of

Josiah, 640–609BC (2 Kings 23:21–23). It was kept through the second temple period, 530BC–AD70. Josephus and the Talmud report celebration of Passover in Jerusalem in the first century AD. With the destruction of the temple in AD70 the sacrifice of the Passover lamb came to an end, and it was now celebrated only within the family.

7 The substance to be used was blood, not anything else. Blood is life, according to the Old Testament (Leviticus 17:11, 14). Fretheim (page 138) comments: 'It is the life given that provides the life for Israel, not simply the blood as a marker of protection.'

8 Unleavened cakes are meant. They figure in other Old Testament rituals: Leviticus 2:4; 7:12. Verse 11 specifies that the meal is to be eaten in haste. The unleavened bread probably indicates that there wasn't enough time for bread to be allowed to rise. As the recital (or *haggadah*) used at the Jewish Passover meal (or *seder*) tells it: 'The *Matzah* is to remind us that before the dough which our forefathers prepared for bread had time to ferment, the supreme King of kings, the Holy One, praised be He, revealed himself to them and redeemed them.'
'Bitter herbs': later Jewish tradition spiritualized the significance of this as a remembrance of the bitterness of life in slavery. The Passover *haggadah* again: 'The *Maror* [bitter herbs] is to remind us that the Egyptians embittered the lives of our forefathers in Egypt.' The Passover recital then quotes Exodus 1:14.

11 The word for 'haste' includes the sense of fear as well: 'trepidation' or 'hurried flight'.
The Hebrew is *pesach*, 'Passover': in Exodus, it means 'to pass over' or 'to pass by'.

13 The 'sign' is a sign both for Israel and for God.

14 'This day' refers, most probably, to the day of Exodus (15 Nisan) and also to the night of the Passover (the evening between 14 and 15 Nisan).

23 On 'the destroyer', see 2 Sam 24:16. Contrast this with verse 13, 'no plague shall destroy you...', where the same basic Hebrew word is used.

26 Since this feast is a permanent ordinance for Israel, it is vital that its significance is made clear. To assist that, the meaning of the feast is put as a response to a child's question. That tradition is continued today in the Passover *seder*, the Jewish celebration of Passover. The story of the exodus is told by way of question and answer, the children asking the questions. Childs (page 200) says that the answers are 'not simply a report, but above all a confession to the ongoing participation of Israel in the decisive act of redemption from Egypt'.

29 The striking down of the first-born takes us back to 4:23, where it is made clear that this punishment is in retribution for Pharaoh's threat to Israel, God's first-born.

32 Pharaoh's request for a blessing is probably not sarcastic. For the first time he is requesting help from Moses without linking it to the removal of a plague. This stresses Pharaoh's complete surrender—at last—under the weight of this final plague. As Brueggemann puts it: this 'is a positive request that acknowledges that the power for life is now fully under the administration of [God], and conversely, that Pharaoh no longer commands that power for life'.

35 The plundering of the Egyptians adds to this impression: Israel has left the land not as refugees but as victors. Childs notes (page 201) that verses 35 and 36 break the forward momentum of the story, returning to a matter set out previously to summarize it.

# 5 Sinai: In service of a holy God

---

**Aims:**

• To deepen our common prayer life.

• To ponder our common experience of God's salvation.

• To think about God's calling to obedience in relationship with him.

• To respond for ourselves to God's words of grace and of calling.

• To ponder God's holiness and his love and concern for his people, and how these are interrelated.

Chapter 19 is part of the 'Sinai account', which extends from 19:1 through to 24:18. Though we look only at chapter 19 this time, it is only part of a longer narrative. Let's look at the wider context. Within the Sinai account there is law-giving, and there is narrative. Fretheim points out (page 201) that a distinctive of the law-giving in the Sinai account is that it is *enclosed by narrative*. We can put this as follows:

*19:1–25* **Story** *Israel arrives at Sinai; God appears to them*
*20:1–17* **Law** *The ten commandments*
*20:18–21* **Story** *Establishment of Moses' covenant role*
*20:22—23:33* **Law** *More covenant laws*
*24:1–18* **Story** *Sealing of the covenant*

Why are narrative and law-giving so strongly interrelated? Fretheim offers a number of compelling reasons. Here is a summary of some of them.

God acts as *subject* of both narrative and law. He acts in the narrative and gives the law. The law fleshes out our knowledge of, and response to, the God who makes himself known in the narrative, and the narrative gives us a clearer picture of the law-giving God.

Without narrative, law seems just that—law. But, when put into the context of a story, we can see more easily that God's law is essentially *gift*, not burden. What's more, the presence of the story makes law *personal*. It is related to its giver and to those to whom it is given. Law is not an *abstract* thing, but is *integrated* with life. It is not just given; it is given at Sinai, after God's deliverance of his people.

The story gives us—and gave Israel—the *motivation* for keeping the law. Law-keeping is a response to a gracious God. Law is to be kept not because it is right to keep it, but because 'it is for our good always, that God might preserve us alive' (Deuteronomy 6:24). It is the *expression of a relationship* with God.

There is a tension between story and law. Jewish theology speaks of a distinction between *haggadah* and *halakhah*. *Haggadah* is the story-telling tradition. Among its strengths is that it is personal. It is about real people, real events. Among its weaknesses is that it tends to locate God within history. *Halakhah* is the law-giving tradition. Its strength is its absoluteness and clarity. Its weakness is its remoteness and inflexibility, and its tendency, if seen alone, to stress God's otherness and to put law-keeping before God's grace.

Jewish theology calls both of these traditions by the name of *Torah*—the Law. In other words, both are essential. Each complements the other.

But which comes first, story or law? Probably the story. 'The law exists for the sake of the story... God's exodus redemption remains the constitutive event for Israel... The law remains forever grounded in those constitutive events' (Fretheim, page 204). Christians believe that God's *grace* comes first. And this is as true of the Old Testament as of the New. We will see in the Sinai account that the law is given in the context of God's saving acts. First Israel is saved, then God gives them the law to keep, as a response and as a condition of continued blessing.

These thoughts throw up another issue. Exodus 1–18 concentrates upon Israel's predicament and its rescue out of Egypt. It is basically *narrative*. Exodus 19–40 takes place at Sinai, and a good deal of it is law. How do we relate these quite different parts of the same book? At the very least we can say that, in the larger movement of the book also, the story of Israel's redemption comes before the giving of the law and is the *setting* for it. Israel is already God's chosen possession: 4:22–23; 3:7. The law-giving at Sinai does *not* establish the relationship between Israel and God. It already exists. What happens at Sinai is the *outworking* of the 'special relationship' which already exists between God and Israel. Many of the thoughts we have had already about the relationship between story and law also apply, then, to the book of Exodus as a whole.

So the Israelites are God's covenant people before ever they get to Sinai. In fact, the covenant came into existence with God's promises to Abraham and 'to your offspring after you' (Genesis 17:7). So what, then, does 'my covenant' (19:5) refer to? Does it refer to the covenant made with Abraham and his offspring, or to the covenant to be sealed in Exodus 24? The last time Exodus has referred to 'covenant' was at 6:4, 5, where the covenant with Abraham, Isaac and Jacob is meant, and it seems sensible to relate 19:5 to that. On the other hand, it would also seem natural for it to refer on to chapter 24.

Perhaps there is actually no competition here! We need to ask how the covenant with Abraham and the covenant at Sinai relate to each other. Fretheim calls the Sinai covenant a vocational covenant for those who are already God's people. In other words, an outworking of an already existing relationship. More of this next time when we deal with chapter 20.

## Verse-by-verse

1 'On the third new moon' is preferable to 'In the third month', since 'on the very day' most naturally refers to a particular day.

3–6 This passage appears to have a literary unity of its own. It anticipates the action of the next few chapters. Its purpose is to summarize the events of Sinai.

4–5 God's first words to Moses here are to remind him of what God has done for the people in rescuing them. The movement we explored in the introduction to Exodus is present here: salvation *out of slavery* to Egypt and *into service* of God.

Note the imagery of verse 4: the strength of the eagle and the tenderness of Israel's home-coming to God.

Note also the order of things. First, God reminds Israel that he has rescued them. Secondly, he reminds them that they have seen this deliverance. They are, together, as a people, witnesses of God's saving acts. Then, and only then, follows the requirement of obedience. This is stressed by the 'now therefore' of verse 5. And, even then, it is not simply a matter of dutiful response: their obedience will be attended by signs of God's favour and grace. For the first time Israel has followed Abraham's example of obedience as a people. It is as a people that they have seen, that they must obey, that they will respond, and that they will be blessed.

6 'Although the whole earth is mine': note the contrast between God's lordship of all of creation and his specific choice of Israel to be his treasured possession. The sheer gift involved in this choice is stressed by the contrast.

'... A kingdom of priests and a holy nation...': there is a parallelism (two similar but slightly different phrases set side by side) here in the Hebrew: 'a kingdom-of-priests and a people-of-holiness'. Israel is a 'kingdom of priests' in that it is to function as mediator between God and the other nations. They are to be a 'holy nation' in that they are set aside for a particular purpose.

8 The significance of Israel's response should not be limited by what follows at Sinai. The ordering of the story is important here. The commandments of chapter 20 follow this response. So does the actual sealing of the covenant in chapter 24. So we must interpret this verse without them for the moment. Israel's response here must be related to what has transpired in verses 4–6 without reference to the Sinai commandments. In other words, obeying God's voice is a wider and deeper matter than keeping the commandments alone. Thus 19:8 is an 'open-ended commitment to God' (Fretheim, page 212).

9 Here we start off on a series of words which convey the majesty and holiness of God. The 'dense cloud' shrouds God from sight, but also expresses his presence. The discussion in the session 2 leader's notes is relevant here. The cloud serves both to reveal and to conceal God. Here, the appearance of God in the cloud conveys to the people God's otherness and serves to support Moses' authority.

10 'Consecrate': the Hebrew root of this verb is the same as that for 'holy' in verse 6. It is also found in verses 14 and 22. The root of the word is the common word for 'holy'. The purpose of this repetition and of all the cloud/smoke/fire/thunder/lightning imagery is to stress the holiness or otherness of God.

Clothes must be washed, sexual relations must be abstained from (verse

15), all as a ritual sign of the specialness of a meeting with a holy God.

19 The verbs have an iterative sense: 'As the blast of the trumpet grew louder and louder, Moses would speak and God would answer him in thunder.'

Here we get the other side of the absence/presence coin. All the imagery so far has stressed the holiness, the otherness of God. God cannot be contained or tamed. Yet, for all that, here he is, talking with Moses, present with his people. The passage is designed to convey the idea of both the presence of God and his awesomeness. To hold both of these ideas together prevents Israel—and us—from either domesticating God (too much presence) or seeing him as irrelevant or too distant (too much absence).

'Thunder' (NRSV); 'the voice of God' (NIV): the meaning is ambiguous. The Hebrew says merely that God answered 'in a voice'. Verse 9 anticipates that God will speak. Clearly verse 19 is meant to be the fulfilment of that. The original does not specify whether God spoke in words or whether any such words were audible. The point is that the people heard God and Moses conversing.

# 6 Exodus 20:1–18
# Sinai: God's terms of service

## Aims

• To reflect how God comes first in salvation and discipleship

• To examine our church life and mission in the light of this and the ten commandments.

• To ponder the relationship between activity and rest under God and to apply this to our lives.

• To consider how Christians are to approach the ten commandments.

• To explore various ethical issues through the ten commandments.

At the end of the study notes, people are asked to ponder before the next meeting what they have gained from their exploration of the book of Exodus. They should then be in a position to share some of that together at the beginning of the seventh session. You may want to remind the group of this, so that they can prepare to do so.

## Overview

There are several Old Testament passages similar to the ten commandments: Exodus 34:17–26; Deuteronomy 27:15–26; Leviticus 19. But the only *parallel* passage is Deuteronomy 5:6–21, the re-giving of the ten commandments at the

89

border of the Promised Land.

Yet our passage stands apart even from Deuteronomy 5—the commandments of Exodus 20 are God's direct address to Israel: verses 1–2. These verses have a double function. They point both backwards and forwards. First, 'I am the Lord, who brought you out...' points back to the rescue out of Egypt. The Lord is a God who acts in fulfilment of his promises. This backwards look refers to 6:2–8, where God promises to rescue his people, and reminds Israel that this promise has been fulfilled. But verses 1–2 also point Israel forwards to a new stage in the relationship between God and his people. Salvation does not stop at Israel's release from Egypt. Salvation extends into a *new relationship between God and his people*. And the ten commandments are the terms on which that relationship is to be built and to grow.

The ten commandments provide the basis for the covenant with all of Israel. One of the roles of the ten commandments is to chart the boundaries of the covenant. That is why the negative commandments concern extreme examples of wickedness. To break them is to step outside the life of God's people. On the other hand, there are positive commandments as well (verses 8–12). They show that the ten commandments also provide positive content for life within the covenant. The existence of positive commandments encourages the reader to see the positive sides of the negative ones also; indeed, to see that each commandment has its positive and its negative. This insight is important for our Christian understanding of the commandments.

There are differences between Exodus 20 and Deuteronomy 5, set out verse-by-verse below. It is clear from them that, though the ten commandments are special, they are not the last word. They were 'not transmitted in a never-to-be-changed form' (Fretheim, page 220). The version in Exodus 20 is already an expanded version of the original words, which were probably short prohibitions. In other words, the explanations for some of the commandments (verses 5–6, 10–11) are likely to be later expansions. This is particularly so for the sabbath commandment, where the differences between Exodus 20 and Deuteronomy 5 are clear. Why did the original commandments get expanded like this? Perhaps they originally served as the basis for homily, exhortation and instruction, and some of the words added in explanation were later included in the text of the commandments themselves.

Both the length of some of the commandments and the brevity of others demonstrate that the ten commandments had, in their original context, a wide scope. The long sabbath commandment goes into detail and then ties down its provisions to some of the principles behind the creation. You can't get much wider than that! The short commandments, because brief and general, also potentially cover a wide range of circumstances.

But we shall see that the ten commandments are not supposed to be remote ethical statements, existing in a kind of vacuum. They aren't supposed to be comprehensive in their detail. They do not say it all. Why is this so, and what implications does it have for our reading of the ten commandments today?

## The pre-Christian role of the ten commandments

First, the ten commandments are found in a particular, concrete historical setting, that of Sinai. We have already explored how this law-giving is bounded by story (see last time's leaders' notes). We find the same point again in 20:2: 'I am the Lord your God who brought you out...'. These laws are unlike, say, commandments found in the Qur'an, the Muslim scriptures. Apart from its supposed transmission to Muhammad, the Qur'an is not given a historical context. This is. The ten commandments are not timeless—they are context-related. So the context in which they are to be grasped—our context—also becomes important.

Secondly, already by Deuteronomy 5 the ten commandments have been open to reworking and expansion as Israel tried to apply them to changing circumstances. At the border of the Promised Land, the ten commandments have already to be seen in a different light and grasped in a different way. Because our context is different from that of historical Israel, that is so for us too. Deuteronomy 5 'gives the people of God in every age an innerbiblical warrant to expand on' the ten commandments (Fretheim, page 222). Of course, we are not to do this randomly or arbitrarily: the New Testament will show us the way forward here.

So the ten commandments are broad but not exhaustive in their scope. They are wide enough to be brought to bear on a variety of situations; but their very width means that they have to be applied to those situations or contexts. They are not detailed regulations, but *principles*, 'open-ended, continually responsive to changing situations in life' (Fretheim, page 224). Israel had to work at applying of the ten commandments to its developing life. So must we.

## Approaching the ten commandments as Christians

To what extent do these guidelines or principles apply to Christians? How are we to apply them to our lives as individuals and as a community? As Christians, we can only approach them through the lens of the New Testament. Jesus' approach to the Law has affected the way we must see things.

There are two different strands in Jesus' approach to the Law. First, he saw the ten commandments as the revealed will of God for his people: Matthew 5:17–20; 19:16–22; 15:4f. Yet Jesus also insisted on a complete freedom towards the Law: see Mark 2:27; 7:15.

Most notably, Jesus *summarizes* the Law. In Matthew 22:34–40 and Mark 12:29–30 he quotes from Deuteronomy 6 and Leviticus 19 and encapsulates the Law in terms of love for God and love for neighbour. Jesus is moving away from any idea that you express your relationship with God by keeping a series of stipulations. He is saying that the principle of love for God and for others is primary. It controls and informs our understanding and implementation of God's will as revealed in the ten commandments.

Paul refers to the ten commandments in Romans 13:8f. There, too, we find that the principle of love has fulfilled the Law. For other New Testament uses of the ten commandments, see James 2:11; Hebrews 4:4, 10.

It is sometimes more difficult to carry out this principle of love than it seems. What about, for example, where two possible acts of love appear to conflict? A pregnant woman scared stiff she cannot cope comes for an abortion. Is it right to show her love by acceding to her request? Would that be an act of love to her anyway? Or should love be shown to the foetus by refusing her? In difficult ethical cases, talk of love doesn't always get us very far down the road towards a practical decision. Perhaps it is particularly then that we need to refer back to passages such as the commandments which support and fill out the detail of this principle of love.

## Verse-by-verse

1   This verse and Deuteronomy 5:1–5 differ. Exodus 20 recounts the original giving of the commandments; Deuteronomy 5 is their retelling at the borders of the land.

2   The detailed parallels between Exodus 20 and Deuteronomy 5:6 start here with God's self-introduction.

3   The fact that this commandment is in 'pole position' indicates its importance. Generally the first commandments relate to God, and the later commandments relate to dealings with other people.

'Before me': various possibilities for translating the Hebrew: 'beside me', 'before me', 'in defiance of me', 'to my disadvantage'. But the overall meaning is clear. It is all about loyalty to God.

4   Paralleled by Deuteronomy 5:8.

5   'I am a jealous God': See Exodus 34:14; Deuteronomy 6:14f; Joshua 24:19f.

'Punishing children...': difficult verses! Cole points out that the natural consequences of hating God can extend to future generations. Childs notes the contrast between the four-generation effect of God's jealousy and the thousand-generation effect of his covenant love. Miller (*Deuteronomy*, page 77) suggests first that the formula is a 'limitation clause', meaning that punishment will go no further than the third and fourth generation; secondly, it is implied that, if the children repent,

God will forgive. Finally, Israel did not uniformly accept the harshest reading of this text: see Deuteronomy 24:16, Ezekiel 18 and Jeremiah 31:29–30. We must read Exodus 20:5 and Deuteronomy 5:9 alongside these other passages.

7 Translations vary. NRSV: 'You shall not make wrongful use of the name of the Lord...'. NIV: 'You shall not misuse the name...'. GNB: 'Do not use my name for evil purposes...'. JB: 'You shall not utter the name of Yahweh your God to misuse it...'. AV: 'Thou shalt not take the name of the LORD thy God in vain...'. Childs: 'You shall not abuse the name...'. NJPS (a Jewish version): 'You shall not swear falsely by the name...'. The words may have a wider range of meaning than just the formal taking of oaths.

Until now, the first person (I, me) has been used for God. From now on, the third person is used.

8 Most of the commandments are in negative terms ('You shall not...'). But this and that in verse 12 are put in positive terms.

The Hebrew *shabbat* (sabbath) may be derived from 'to rest, cease from work'. Brueggemann (*The Land*, 1977, page 63) comments: 'We have yet to learn of the radical meaning of sabbath for landed people... It is the institutional reminder to Israel that cessation from frantic activity will not cause the world to disintegrate or society to collapse. Sabbath sets a boundary to our best, most intense efforts to manage life...for our security and well-being... Rest is essential to the history of God himself.'

'Keeping it holy': another use of the root 'holy', which we found in chapter 19. This suggests a positive action—making the day holy—rather than simply absence of activity.

10f Deuteronomy 5:14 adds 'so that your manservant and maidservant may rest as you do'. Deuteronomy 5:15 is completely different to Exodus 20:11. The former is a reminder of the exodus itself. The latter explains the sabbath by way of a creation ordinance. The editor of Exodus seems keen to root the keeping of the sabbath in the order of creation. The editor of Deuteronomy has different principles in mind: Israel was a slave; Israel's own servants should be accorded the right to keep the Sabbath. Only that way will all Israel be able to worship God.

12 'Honour' means more than to obey; but to prize highly, to hold in high regard and affection.

Deuteronomy 5:16 adds 'that it may be well with you'.

13 Does this mean 'you shall not kill', or 'you shall not murder'? It probably cannot have a meaning as wide as 'kill', since much else in Old Testament seems to countenance the taking of life. One possibility: what are prohibited are acts of homicidal violence arising out of hatred and malice. In other words, the taking of the law into one's own hands.

17 Different words for 'covet' are used in this verse and in Deuteronomy 5:21. The one used here may emphasize emotion leading to action, whereas the one used in Deuteronomy may stress the emotion itself.

# 7 Covenant and calling

## Aims

• To provide an opportunity, as appropriate, for people to express their desire to serve and obey God more deeply, by means of an act of covenant renewal.

• To reflect, in the group meeting, the movement of the passage from covenant renewal to fellowship meal.

• To take time to relax together, over some kind of meal if you wish!

This chapter brings to completion the sealing of the covenant between God and the children of Israel which was announced in 19:3. Again, this chapter looks backwards and forwards. Backwards to the announcing of the covenant and the giving of the law (chapters 19 and 20), of which this is the culmination. Forwards to the golden calf in chapter 32 and the re-establishment of the covenant in chapter 34 despite Israel's disobedience and idolatry. It is worth noting that this covenant does not guarantee the people's obedience; it merely gives them a basis on which to live in fellowship with God.

The verses probably have a composite structure. Verse 1 does not seem to follow very naturally from the end of chapter 23. The command of verses 1-2 aren't carried out until verses 9-11, and the sealing of the covenant is interposed in verses 3-8. But we are more interested in the way the verses have been put together. The editing makes the act of covenant renewal a two-stage process—*blood-sprinkling* and *covenant meal*. A solemn ceremony at which the covenant is sealed is followed by a fellowship meal with God, when the people are enabled to enjoy the fruit of that covenant—closer communion with God.

The leader's notes for session 5 have already suggested that this isn't a covenant-from-scratch between God and his people. To say that would be to ignore all that happened before with Abraham, Isaac and Jacob. This is a *vocational* covenant, 'a closer specification of what is entailed in [the] relationship [between God and Israel] in view of what Israel has become as a people and in the light of their recent experience' (Fretheim, page 256). This sealing of the covenant is all about the people's loyalty and obedience.

We have done a lot of work over the last few weeks. This is the last session, and you may not want to do much study together. The suggestion is that you follow through in your meeting the same movement as we find in this passage: from covenant-sealing to a

94

time of fellowship expressed by eating together.

## Some practical suggestions

Our study notes incorporate for your use, as you feel appropriate, a covenant renewal ceremony, taken from the Methodist Service Book, 1975. Methodists use it at the turn of the year. *It should be used in a way that does not oblige people to respond or to assent to it if they do not feel ready or able.* If you feel uncertain as to whether your group would be ready to use this ceremony together, why not discuss the issue with them in advance? You might wish to read it out loud to and on behalf of the group, allowing members to assent to it within themselves as they feel able. Or you could move on from a reading of the passage, together with any discussion on it, to a meal or a snack together, and encourage the members to take the study sheets home with them and use the prayer as they want in their personal devotions.

As to the possibility of a meal, do be sensitive to the nature of your group and the time at which it meets. If a full-blown meal is possible, do think about the cost, and whether it should be shared. Perhaps members might each like to bring a savoury or a sweet course with them, so that everyone can share together. This often avoids embarrassment for those on a limited budget.

If your group meets during the day, or is limited in time for any

reason, it may not be possible to have a meal together. You could always have a snack, or bring a cake and share it, or something similar.

One note: The Methodist service book says: 'The traditional words "Put me to doing, put me to suffering" do not mean that we ask God to make us suffer, but that we desire, by God's help, actively to do or patiently to accept whatever is God's will for us.' You may feel it right to explain this to the group before using the prayer.

## Verse-by-verse

3 Commentators differ on how to interpret 'all the Lord's words and laws'. The 'words' may refer to the ten commandments and the 'laws' or 'ordinances' to the supplementary laws recorded at 21:1 onwards. If that is so, then Moses is here recapitulating the law in the context of the covenant renewal ceremony.

The people offer their obedience, twice, here and in verse 7. Note that this is a replay of 19:8. But it is not the same as 19:8. There the people were affirming their desire to obey God before they had heard the law. Here, they state their readiness to obey after hearing the law. So this statement is a more knowing, solemn and deliberate affair than 19:8. The fact that Moses repeats the law before the covenant is sealed shows the solemnity of the occasion.

8 Why use blood? There are other Old Testament texts where covenant and blood are linked. In Genesis 15:17f a covenant is sealed with God passing between the pieces of sacrificed animals. In Jeremiah 34:18 a fate like a dissected calf is offered as a threat for covenant disobedience. Blood may symbolize the

covenant sealed between God and Israel as a means of life. Or it may stand for purification. Whatever the symbolism, the gravity of the ceremony is evident.

10 The words 'and they saw the God of Israel' couldn't be blunter. Yet, even here, God is not described. Instead, we are told what the pavement under his feet looked like. For parallels, see Isaiah 6 and Ezekiel 1. There, though the text talks in terms of 'seeing' God, the following description also moves away from any attempt to describe him. In Isaiah 6, the description is of the throne, etc. In Ezekiel 1, phrases such as 'the appearance of...' or 'what looked like...' fulfil the same function.

11 Eating and drinking makes this ceremony a covenant meal. Childs (page 507): 'These verses... function as a eucharistic festival...'. The links between this passage and holy communion are worth thinking about.

Why is it now possible to see God and to eat and drink with him, when in chapter 19 the dangers of getting too close to him were made very clear? It isn't that God has become less holy or awesome. It is that the sealing of the covenant has made closer communion with him possible.

# Reading Resource List

## Jonah

L.C. Allen, *The Books of Joel, Obadiah, Jonah and Micah*, New International Commentaries on the Old Testament, 1976

D.W. Baker, D. Alexander and B. Waltke, *Obadiah, Jonah, Micah*, Tyndale Old Testament Commentary, 1988

T. Fretheim, *The Message of Jonah*, 1977

G.A.F. Wright and F.W. Golka, *The Song of Songs & Jonah*, International Theological Commentaries, 1988

J.M. Sasson, *Jonah*, The Anchor Bible Commentaries, 1990

H.W. Wolff, *Obadiah and Jonah*, Augsburg Commentaries, 1986

## Exodus

B. Childs, *The Book of Exodus*, Old Testament Library Commentaries, 1974

R.A. Cole, *Exodus*, Tyndale Old Testament Commentaries, 1973

T. Fretheim, *Exodus*, Interpretation Commentaries, 1991

T. Mann, *The Book of Torah*, John Knox, 1988